W9-AKY-210

The Experts Praise

Managing New Products:
Using the MAP™ System to Accelerate Growth,
Third Edition

"The most profound ideas are best communicated with a simple concept. The "MAP" concept is a great example of this principle. It is simple and easy to understand, but extremely profound. Properly applied, "MAP" will fundamentally change a company's approach to and success rate with new products."

—JOHN R. BERSCHIED, JR.
Senior Partner, Lighthouse Group

"Between the covers of *Managing New Products* third edition, Tom Kuczmarski has captured all of the answers to the What, Why and How issues of growth through innovation, new products and new services.

"*Managing New Products* is a "must read" for every business that wants to innovate winning solutions in today's competitive environment.

"The MAP™ construct really covers all the bases and gives clear, pragmatic and actionable prescriptions to all management levels for implementing innovation in your company.

"This millennium will begin with unprecedented forces of technological revolution and total globalization of markets and suppliers destroying our old business models and forging new approaches. *Managing New Products* may be the best change agent available to us today, providing a detailed road map for all levels of management to thoroughly ingrain an innovative posture throughout the organization."

—CARL BOCHMANN
Riverbend Engineering

"Tom Kuczmarski has developed a simple system that injects some common sense into the risky challenge of developing and managing new products. The opening chapters on implementing his MAP System are worth the price of admission alone."

—JOE CAPPO

Senior Vice President—
International and Licensing
Crain Communications, Inc.

———

"There are many books on the market today about growth, and a lot of books about new product development. This book demonstrates the critical link between new product development, innovation and growth, and provides an easy to understand framework for creating a corporate culture that consistently grows through innovative practices."

—ALEX COOPER

Publisher, *Product Development Best Practices Report*

———

"*Managing New Products* is a must read for executives responsible for advancing the product/service offerings of their companies. Success in product development requires discipline and effort. It cannot be left to chance. Tom provides the parameters and guidelines as a roadmap for successful new product journeys. The effort necessary to complete the journey is reduced when you follow Tom's approach."

—TRACY EMERICK

President, Taurus Direct Marketing & Receptive Marketing, Inc.

"Tom's work is the right opener for those who realize they have yet to unleash the full potential of new products in their companies. Superior new products performers become industry leaders, and the elements are all here to construct a leading new products "factory" for your organization."

—MIKE GEARIN

Director, Data Services,
Cincinnati Bell Long Distance

———

"The MAP System is a logical, practical approach to new product development. While many authors cover the development process (one of the "P" tools in the MAP System), this book goes further—bringing in the qualitative factors that can result in the difference between success and failure. Building on the track records of successful new product development companies, Kuczmarski has compiled a comprehensive cell of ideas crucial to the "innovation revolution" of the new millennium. Practitioners will definitely want to have this third edition as part of their libraries!"

—LINDA GORCHELS

Director, Executive Marketing Programs
Executive Education-School of Business,
University of Wisconsin-Madison and author of
The Product Manager's Handbook

———

"Business needs new products, and it's this innovation that will determine a company's ability to thrive and maybe even survive in the new millennium. *Managing New Products* is a practical, sensible guide for creating an environment for product development explaining what it is, how it works and how to make it a repeatable process."

—RICK KEAN,

Executive Director,
Business Marketing Association

"Tom Kuczmarski is the natural person to write crisply and insightfully about the high-risk area of new product development. In his career, he has examined scores of companies' new product approaches and knows the rules of developing and launching successful new products."

—PHILIP KOTLER

Distinguished Professor of
International Marketing
J.L. Kellogg Graduate School of Management,
Northwestern University

———

"Robust New Product Development is the oxygen that feeds the fire of corporate growth. Kuczmarski's MAP System is a great road map to guide and sustain such processes so that new product ideas bear fruit for the benefit of all the firm's stakeholders."

—ALLAN J. MAGRATH

Director Corporate Marketing and New Business
Ventures, 3M Canada Company

———

"After really understanding how important the growth role was for new products, we committed fully to the "development process" with a team of "senior managers and new product champions." We are off to a great start and with the MAP™ process for our template, we are anticipating much success!"

—JOSEPH MILLER

Vice Chairman, Oil-Dri Corporation of America

"Mature American businesses are searching for what once made them great. The shareholder has reaped the benefit of quality and re-engineering. The imperative for profitable growth is upon us. The contribution of innovation and new product development must be understood and the risk concern rationalized against future opportunity. The book *Managing New Products* by Tom Kuczmarski and the MAP System therein help set the framework for growth. It's working for us, I recommend it."

—ROBERT E. PUISSANT

Senior Vice President—Marketing & Strategic Planning, WICOR Energy Group

———

"Forget line extensions. The future belongs to companies that innovate with truly new products. Thomas Kuczmarski's innovative management system will show you the way."

—AL RIES

Chairman, Ries & Ries

———

"Successful new products are inspiration and perspiration. Tom Kuczmarski's MAP approach systemizes the inspiration and reduces the perspiration. It's a winner!"

—DON E. SCHULTZ

Professor, Northwestern University and President, Agora, Inc.

"Sustained innovation is *the* key strategy for success in consumer products—and no one understands innovation better than Tom Kuczmarski. This new edition does an even better job of bringing together all the elements of successful innovation.

"While no one can guarantee success on any particular project, a good development process based on the right principles can virtually assure eventual success. The MAP™ System is the best total approach to innovation-focused development I have seen. It comprehends the fundamental nature of innovation, lays out key principles and best practices, defines a clear process and outlines the roles of all the key players, including senior management. It should help not only understanding the innovation process—but also, importantly, help get it done.

"I appreciated the comprehensive treatment of innovation, rather than the more anecdotal approaches I typically see. I believe the MAP™ System can help even the most experienced development manager or executive."

—DANNY L. STRICKLAND
Senior Vice President, Innovation,
Technology & Quality, General Mills

———

"The MAP System is the most powerful tool for enhancing corporate value that I have seen in years!"

—TYLER K. COMANN
Partner, Comann & Montague

———

"This book is an outstanding read for any top manager. Tom Kuczmarski does a brilliant job at delineating the critical success factors that can significantly enhance the productivity of your new product efforts."

—H. FISK JOHNSON, PH.D.
Vice Chairman, S.C. Johnson & Son, Inc.

Managing New Products

Using the MAP™ System to Accelerate Growth

THIRD EDITION

Thomas D. Kuczmarski

THE INNOVATION PRESS
Book Ends Publishing
Chicago, Illinois

Library of Congress Cataloging-in-Publication Data
available from the Library of Congress.

Published by The Innovation Press of
Book Ends Publishing
430 W. Roslyn Place
Chicago, IL 60614
Copyright © 2000 by Thomas D. Kuczmarski

All rights reserved. No part of this book may be reproduced,
stored in a retrieval system, or transmitted in any form
or by any means, electronic, mechanical, photocopying,
recording, or otherwise, without the prior
written permission of Book Ends Publishing.
Printed in the United States of America
ISBN: 0-9677817-0-1

To Susan Smith Kuczmarski,
Educator, Innovator, and Partner,
and to my sons, John, James, and Thomas

Contents

Part III
The Process

Part IV
The People

Acknowledgments

I would like to express my sincere thanks and gratitude to my partner in life, Dr. Susan Smith Kuczmarski. She is my soulmate who continues to provide me with inspiration and support.

Many other people have helped in the development of this third edition. I am especially appreciative of their commitment, dedication, support and hard work. I give them my most gracious thanks. They include Rich Hagle, Eva Malecki, Adoleena A. Plunkett, John Kaminski, Eric Lochner, Carl Bochmann and Francesca Van Gorp Cooley.

Preface

Over the years I had written numerous articles on the subject of managing new products and had learned a great deal from students and faculty in teaching new products and services, international marketing, and marketing policy at Northwestern University's Kellogg Graduate School of Management. I had many requests from business executives as well as business school professors to compile the writings and consulting experiences into a book. The result was the first edition of this book, in which I identified the factors that influence new product success by observing the common patterns and threads that cut across companies most successful at commercializing new products. The second edition was updated to reflect new practices and changes in the marketplace.

Since the second edition of *Managing New Products* was published eight years ago, I have interviewed and worked with scores of companies—both good and bad at new product development and innovation. I have attempted to incorporate many of my observations and lessons learned into this third edition. The feedback from readers and, most important, from new product practitioners has been overwhelmingly positive. It seems that many of the ideas and approaches described in this book tend to be in the minds of many managers but often remain unspoken.

Managing New Products: Using The MAP™ *System to Accelerate Growth* provides the reader a unique framework for developing successful new products and services. It enables an executive to view the company's processes and resources from a new innovative perspective. In this third edition, I have made several revisions that are aimed at updating as well as clarifying some key elements of the book.

I still fervently believe that CEOs and senior managers must focus more time, attention, and resources on new products in order to realize long-term benefits from them. Without this necessary dose of top management commitment, managers receive mixed signals on the expectations and roles that new products will play in the future growth plans of the company. If CEOs and division presidents totally abdicate new product responsibility, managers may wander aimlessly through a maze of new products without reaching consensus on the key candidates for commercialization. Top management must provide a vision for the future role of new products to help support and guide internal new product activities. I hope that you will pass a copy of this book on to *your* senior managers so they can read for themselves how to be more effective at new product development.

Over twenty years ago, when I was a new areas brand manager at the Quaker Oats Company, I searched for guidelines on developing new products and would have welcomed a book like this one. While a few textbooks outlined a development process, I could not find anything that described how to increase the success rate of internally developed new products. Most of the literature talked about statistical models and quantitative tests aimed at reducing the risks of commercialization. Simulated market tests seemed to be "in" as research firms conveyed an ability to predict first-year sales for a new product with a high degree of accuracy.

These financially oriented and process-driven approaches for managing a new products program left me cold. What were the real success factors that separated the winners from the losers? During my tenure at Booz Allen & Hamilton, I began to address this issue. I worked with several companies to assist them in improving their success rates in new products and I also directed the firm's study on best practices in new product management. Overall, the study surveyed the new product management practices of over seven hundred companies that introduced thirteen thousand new products during a five-year period. As part of that study, I conducted personal interviews with executives at over one hundred companies to discern the underlying factors that drove new product performance. The study represented the largest database ever established on how companies manage new products. The Booz Allen publication, *New Products Management for the 1980s,* received widespread interest and publicity. More than ten thousand requests poured in for copies of this publication. Why? Because the study uncovered key qualitative factors that are instrumental to new product success.

During the past sixteen years, Kuczmarski & Associates Inc., an innovation management consulting firm specializing in new product development, branding strategy, and growth planning, has afforded me the opportunity to understand in further depth the success formula for new product management. The majority of our clients have had successful results in new products within a relatively short period of time. However, much of my thinking since I was at Booz Allen has changed. Managing my own business—a new product in and of itself—offers a perspective on the subject that a large corporation could never provide. Profound similarities exist between successful entrepreneurship and successful new product management in large corporations. Infusing entrepreneurship into a corporation's new product culture is one essential ingredient for success.

Why read this book?

This book is intended for top management and new product managers. Regardless of the size of the organization, these two players represent the nucleus of any new product development program. One cannot succeed without the support of the other. Therefore, this book is directed at two levels of management within a company: top managers who have the power to make change occur, and the line managers who are involved in and responsible for new product development results. Both levels of management need to be on board. A dedicated team of new product managers cannot be successful without top management's commitment and support. Nor can top management execute a successful new product program without a dedicated and talented team of new product people. The two work hand in hand with each other.

Thus, this book is aimed at identifying for top managers the critical factors that shape a successful new product development program. For new product managers, it is intended to serve as a handbook on developing new products successfully. A new product blueprint, a strategy, and a development process are the basic tools needed to set the stage for innovation. The new product blueprint outlines the direction to take. The new product strategy is the cornerstone for a successful process, since it identifies the game plan for knowing how to get there. And the development process represents the road map, which is followed by a multidisciplinary mix of product champions and functional managers. This book describes how to blend creativity with analysis to identify new product concepts. The approaches suggested will breathe creativity into many bureaucratic corridors of U.S. corporations and spark innovation.

If you see no growth role for new products in your own company, then you need to read this book even more carefully than the company that recognizes new products as a key source of future growth. For while acquisitions can be a very appropriate growth mode to augment new products, companies that tend to focus all of their growth funds and management talent on acquisitions are usually poor new product developers. So you can either continue to buy companies, wait for the potential of existing product lines to materialize, hope internal management will discover some new growth finds, or make some major changes in the way your company manages innovation and new product development.

If you should decide that your corporation's best interests lie in launching new products, this book will provide a holistic approach to new product activities. We present in this third edition a new framework called the MAP™ System. This new way of thinking about the success requirements for new products and services will be prescriptive for all managers in the 21st century. In addition, this book will discuss the culture most likely to aid a corporation in its quest for successful new products.

Innovation will fuel the future strength of the global economy. Those corporations that do not innovate may not survive. The corporations that are making it are those that are able to accommodate change, that strive to create an entrepreneurial culture for their employees—in short, corporations that can and do innovate. Successful new product management requires that top management and internal product champions maintain a consistent level of commitment to the new product effort. In light of the financial, performance, and time demands on management, maintaining new product commitment does take guts.

The MAP™

Too many corporate executives work at cross-purposes. On one hand, they say—and tell members of their corporate team—that they want innovative approaches to their new product development programs. Then they follow by encouraging the same people to avoid risk. Such "encouragement" may come in the form of directives to avoid risky propositions and to concentrate on "company strengths," which means line extensions. Or it may come indirectly in the form of impossible processes that discourage any new project except a "sure thing."

As this section demonstrates, there are no sure things. But there are ways to ensure that risks are measured and managed in ways that increase the possibility of success and, equally important, that maximize the potential of the really big winners. The MAP System™ is especially valuable because it draws on the practices and processes that most companies already have or use. Like a traditional map it provides the ability to set a course and make adjustments along the way to, in this case, new product success.

CHAPTER 1

The Need for Innovation

I*t is a rare company that can escape the impact of today's rapidly shifting markets and expanding technology. Existing products can be expected, in the course of time, either to be preempted by new and improved products or to degenerate into profitless price competition. Only through continually bringing forth new products can most manufacturing companies sustain their long-run growth and profitability.*

Reprinted by permission of the *Harvard Business Review.* Excerpt from "How to Organize for New Products" by Samuel C. Johnson and Conrad Jones (May/ June 1957). Copyright 1957 by the President and Fellows of Harvard College, all rights reserved.

Are innovative new products a good way to grow a business? Or to reinvigorate a mature one? Where were you during the 1990s, when totally new companies and industries were invented, broken apart and invented again? When Microsoft, a company that didn't exist a generation ago, and others replaced some of the venerable old-line members of the Dow? And when the U.S. auto industry recaptured lost markets and made impressive inroads into new markets with its new products?

Of course, the power of new products and potential returns can be enormous. But there are risks, risks that seem larger than those of other growth strategies. At least that's how many corporate executives see it. New product innovation simply *looks* more risky than line extensions, acquisitions and licensing agreements. And executives get paid for making profits, not for taking risks. Unfortunately, the financial community has continued to emphasize extremely short-term horizons; in effect, three months. Such shortsightedness will be the death knell for innovation if it continues. It sets up an internal environment that perpetuates constant reallocation of resources—often away from new product and R&D efforts.

In contrast to popular beliefs, investing in new product development *can* increase stock price. Our firm recently conducted a study of best practices in innovation from over 200 companies. Over 75 percent of the best companies cited "new products and services have contributed greatly to our stock price during the past five years." Moreover, compared to the top three competitors, 72 percent of the best organization's stock price was significantly greater as a result of new product success within their organization.

These research statistics certainly support the premise that innovation indeed *can* drive stock price. While other growth strategies may be used, virtually all companies use new product innovation to some degree as a core component of their business strategy. Innovation can offer a real longer-term competitive and sustainable advantage for companies. *Innovative* is the adjective that will differentiate a successful company in the future from its less successful competitors.

What is New Product Innovation?

So what is innovation? In the simplest terms, externally, it is "offering a new perceived benefit to a customer; a change." Internally, new product innovation is the set of functional skills required to conceive, develop, and bring a new product or service to profitable realization. Innovation provides genuine "newness" to an organization's customers or constituency. Further, it is a mindset, an all-consuming attitude that drives the way managers think about business strategies, processes, leadership,

and structures. It is analogous to continuous process improvement in that it is an attitude that feeds on and sustains itself.

It should be easy to see that innovation thrives in an environment that uses analytical tools to measure and manage creative endeavors. Successful new product innovation is the
result of the deliberate assessment of market needs and a company's internal strengths and abilities to meet those needs.
Success is not the result of "mysterious" forces and impulses
but, rather, the application of disciplined techniques. Like any
skill, discipline needs to be "exercised" to improve it. The
more it is used, the more it produces greater ability and confidence, which in turn produces a higher than normal success
rate. This reinforces the mindset that produces success. In
short, practice makes perfect.

Risk, Growth, and New Product Innovation

Top management often equates new products and new services
with high risk. Of course new products are risky. If one begins
or introduces something new, there is bound to be a degree of
uncertainty in its outcome and acceptance. But the relative degree of risk can be managed and balanced. Scarred by past failures, management is often inclined to run scared and drop the
new product ball when the team has hardly had time to practice. Top management begins to ask, "What's the return that we
can expect from this new product investment? Why should we
continue to funnel dollars into this high-risk, bottomless pit?"
Consequently, managers become more and more inclined to
focus on "me-too" products rather than take the risks to develop truly innovative ones. Among the many barriers to risk-
taking are the following:

   ✧ Risk-averse settings where failure in new prod-
     ucts is unacceptable and entrepreneurial product
     champions are not recognized or encouraged
   ✧ No road map to frame new product concept
     development

◈ Inadequate funding behind new products

◈ Management focusing on *projects* rather than setting up a new product strategy and process

◈ Reward and incentive systems geared to near-term profitability rather than new product performance

Line extensions can serve very valuable new product and business strategies, but they are among the most abused marketing tactics employed today in the name of "new product development." Truly new products deliver truly new benefits. But product managers tend to wrongly rely on them as remedies for risk. They tend to think that risk can be avoided with these "sure things" that involve a simple tweak to an existing, worn-out product with a claim that it's "new and improved" and then offer it on discount. What could be safer?

Risk aversion leads to the same tired old line extensions that have become legendary in the packaged goods industry. After all, what risk could one more "new and improved" size, color or shape create? A risk-free quick hit? How about, as more and more companies have found out, confused customers, alienated retailers, glutted inventory, cannibalized product lines, and skyrocketing handling costs? Warned for years about problems with the traditional brand management system, consumer packaged goods companies have relied on mindlessly churning out meaningless product variations. Consequently, they have lost their customers' loyalty to retailers such as Wal-Mart.

Managers get a false sense of security because line extensions feel safe and easy. But in today's competitive global markets, where a customer can compare prices and features from producers all over the world at the touch of a keypad, most so-called "sure things" are extinct. Moreover, they further rationalize that keeping the ship afloat today is more important than sailing to parts unknown tomorrow.

Firefighting will always be part of business management, but the key is to strike a balance between managing today's business and tomorrow's new products. However, the power of new products *is* understood by many successful executives. So the obvious question emerges, How can corporations exploit the positive power of new products while limiting the degree of risk and potential loss? The answer: by having the guts to *take* the risks and demonstrate the commitment to provide the resources. The rest—process—can be learned.

Acquisitions Are Risky, Too

For the past thirty years, many corporations have opted for heavy doses of acquisitions as their growth medicine. Management across many industries perceives acquisitive growth as a lower-risk approach compared to developing new products internally. "You know what you are getting for your dollars when you buy an ongoing business," says the president of a three-billion-dollar food company.

A Canadian products analyst comments on the need to be associated with a big brand name in order to compete on the shelves of a store: "Given the increasing number of new product introductions, there's a great deal of competition for shelf space, so you can't afford to have the number 10 brand sitting here.

Why did the RJR Nabisco merger fail in the end? In 1985, this marriage of the number-two cigarette maker and the number-four U.S. food company promised to create the largest United States-based consumer products company. Nabisco was to benefit by gaining access to more money for advertising, and RJR saw the merger as a way to continue its diversification into non-tobacco business ventures. In the end, though, RJR Nabisco's shareholders wanted to establish a clear boundary between the food and tobacco operations, so they voted to split the company into roughly its original forms. In the end, the desire to expand backfired because of the antipathy of different customer types.

And the list of acquisition failures goes on and on. Yet for some strange reason, many top managers in this country are naively enamored with acquisition as their best tool for growth. It is an immediate gratification. Perhaps acquisitions act as a pacifier for some corporate leaders. Yet while buying up other companies may offer instant power and an ego trip, in the long run, acquisitions and new product development carry similar kinds of risk.

Short of a change in government policy or attitude toward acquisitions, major corporations will continue to seek out the "hot" growth companies. They will be forced to buy other companies for growth if they don't give innovation a shot. As corporations grow older and larger, they tend to gain weight, become sluggish, and show signs of "arthritis" in their decision making. They prefer to stick to products they are comfortable with and concentrate on "yeah, buts" rather than "what ifs." Unless companies are willing to commit to developing new products internally, no major growth options exist other than acquisition or joint venture.

As small entrepreneurial businesses continue to sprout, large corporations will have a future source of supply for acquisitions. At some point, however, it will be recognized that in order to maintain the entrepreneurship in these companies and their corresponding success, the acquiring company must yield to innovation. Placing an entrepreneurial, fast-growing company into the shroud of corporate bureaucracy is usually a sure-fire way of stifling the growth patterns previously enjoyed. Moreover, the acquisition price for small companies will likely increase as entrepreneurs come to understand that they have something many corporations won't achieve internally.

Acquisitions have proven repeatedly to have no built-in success formula. Companies take risks and win and lose at both acquisitions *and* new products. Acquisition is not the be-all-and- end-all solution to growth and diversification. Yet acquisitions are indeed viable growth alternatives. So, innovation—that is, starting something new—can often be far more profitable than acquisitions. The amazing and explosive growth of internet companies certainly demonstrates the potential value of starting a new business or service.

The New Competitor— Small Start-Ups

While acquiring high-potential startups may provide legitimate sources for growth, the ability to launch new products that are internally developed will provide more control over a corporation's desired growth. Internal new product development enables a company to be in the driver's seat—setting the direction offensively for growth that a company wants to take. With acquisitions, one has to choose from available candidates, which may or may not fit the company. Some companies wait for years before the right acquisition comes along.

While examples abound of big corporations that have demonstrated a successful track record in developing new products, most need to examine some of the exemplary approaches, styles, and directions taken by small companies. Corporations need to rebuild the entrepreneurial pilings that often become splintered and decayed over time. Corporate hierarchical management layers and a flurry of memos will not cure the problem. If the model for U.S. companies to follow in the past was Japanese companies, the model to follow today is the small company down the street from the sprawling corporate office. "Click" companies (internet-related or computer-based companies/services) are clearly out performing our mainline "brick" companies (manufacturing companies).

Companies complain about loss of market share, yet they seem reluctant to compete head to head by developing truly new products that will provide a sustainable competitive edge. Rather, they often choose "safe" approaches: increase trade deals and advertising support, drop the price, and expand the distribution channels. How long does it take for competition to respond to or duplicate these types of moves? Not long. And worse, what they do in the short term is often counterproductive in the long term. In the few years surrounding the turn of the last century, the U.S. produced a remarkable number of inventions, ranging from the light bulb and automobile to the telephone and radio—innovations that totally changed people's lives. Will the turn of the new century and millennium produce a similar level of innovation? I think it's evident that we already have entered an *innovation revolution*. It's not a fad. It's here to stay for 20 to 30 years. So, don't avoid it. Accept it.

This book will present approaches that successful companies have used to capture the talent and rekindle an innovative mindset. By keeping a bank of talented motivated product champions, companies can innovate within the confines of their existing corporate fences. In order to make successful new products happen, U.S. corporations have to be willing to take more risks and treat people as entrepreneurs.

The MAP™ System

I've created a new framework that companies of all sizes can use to accelerate new product innovation. This framework can be viewed as an organic system that creates a culture to encourage and perpetuate people to take risks and go after big ideas—to be more innovative than ever before.

Innovative new products don't happen by accident. They are the result of a disciplined approach to managing creativity and newness. Innovative new product development can be seen as involving three core skills (*Measure, Manage, Motivate*) and three essential tools (*Plan, Process, People*) linked by the right attitude or innovative mindset. Each skill and tool work interdependently with each other.

The linchpin to the system is A for *Attitude*. This means attitude toward *Risk* because there is no real new product invention without risk and there is no success without the elements of the MAP™. Each component of the MAP™ system is critical to *innovation* success. A summary of each component follows.

Measure

Starting with the belief that you can't manage what you can't measure, my colleagues and I have developed innovation metrics that measure the entire range of new product effectiveness. It's critical to evaluate and measure various milestones along the development cycle. Measuring your return on innovation *is* key but several other dimensions of the process also are important—from measuring and assessing customer need, to monitoring the new product development pipeline flow, to assessing new product team effectiveness and motivation. Measurement is needed to determine how well you're doing before you ever get to the market. Once you've launched a product, it's fairly easy to measure performance at that point. It all boils down to dollars and cents. Similarly, the processes being used should be measured to determine whether the plan is on target or not. Employee performance and perceptions also should be measured as a means of establishing reward and motivation strategies.

Manage

This area is probably the greatest source of nervousness for senior managers—and the greatest source of confusion. Namely, the belief that innovation is some sort of mysterious "creative" process that can't be managed. New product innovation comes from intimate knowledge of customer wants and needs and a disciplined approach to developing solutions that reflect and anticipate those needs and wants. Further rigor in assessing the profit potential, and greater discipline in testing and evaluation according to clearly stated criteria helps to separate emotional fervor from rational opportunity. As identification of customer needs are developed and refined, the "fuzzy front end" is adjusted—that is, *managed*—by the use of various kinds of criteria in line with desired outcomes. The cross-functional teams dedicated to executing the plan of course must be managed. The old saying about genius being 99 percent perspiration and 1 percent inspiration is never more true.

Motivate

A culture of innovation includes both the intangible "soft" incentives, such as positive feedback and team structures that encourage employees to embrace risk, and "hard incentives," such as reward systems that enable employees to benefit from intelligent risk-taking. The corporate culture should encourage (or motivate) all team members to contribute to the development of the innovation plan and make sure that norms and values are in place to support it.

Attitude

This is the linchpin of the entire new product innovation process. In a time when virtually any item can be purchased instantly over the internet, the technology of new product development, while extremely valuable and vitally important, is in many respects the easy part. The hard part is creating a mindset that supports risk-taking and personal self-esteem building. Many "state-of-the-art" companies fail miserably because they lack the necessary culture, leadership, and teamwork. The attitude or mindset is what inspires and feeds, or limits and constrains, individual spirit and creativity.

Plan

Technology tends to get all the attention, but planning (or strategy) is the one tool that most consistently points the way to breakthrough new products. Wal-Mart is a classic example. While they use sophisticated buying procedures and just-in-time inventory tactics, they also outsmart the competition by choice of location and service and appeal to customers in unusual ways. For example, while virtually all companies actively discourage overnight parking in their parking lots, Wal-Mart actively encourages R-Vers to use their parking lots for overnight parking—much to the chagrin of their competitors, who are scrambling to show how "customer-friendly" they are.

Another example is Continental Airlines, long considered an also-ran in the airline industry. An early 1999 *Wall Street Journal* article reported that the airline had become the leading operator in the New York City area. It had gained more than three percent increase in market share over an 18-month period, an enormous change. It simply made Newark Airport a hub, which enabled it to offer better and faster service to busy commuters. The strategy didn't involve a single new piece of technology; just more of what customers wanted, which is the essence of every smart strategic plan.

Process

Every time someone says, "I've seen it all," with respect to new technology, a new development makes the speaker take the statement back. The digital and electronic revolution of the second half of the twentieth century has been one of the marvels of human history. Innovations in technology have led to unbelievable changes in how people work and what they can produce. And the changes have been qualitative as well as quantitative.

Process improvements, technology-based and otherwise, such as mass customization and concurrent engineering, which have been discussed at length in many books, have produced increasingly shorter cycle times, faster speed to market, and quantum increases in productivity. While it is impossible to imagine what new developments await us, it is almost equally impossible to imagine what else can be done or, more to the point, what we as consumers, can absorb and assimilate into our lives. Numerous technological innovations suffered from being ahead of their time. Nevertheless, the improvements keep coming.

Technological innovations can be deceptive because they feel "easy" relative to such strategies as employee development. Technology, no matter how smart or sophisticated, is only as good as its application—by well-trained, compensated, and motivated individuals—and its uses. Incorporating new processes, technologically based or not, should include potential changes to overall plans and to the company culture.

People

People still execute the plans and make the processes work efficiently. That means morale is as important as ever, maybe more so. Hewett & Associates has adopted an unusual approach. After 15 years (and every subsequent five years), an employee gets a "splash"—a five-week sabbatical. The only restriction is that the individual must work or study or otherwise participate in a non-expertise area. Thus, a consultant who is a distribution specialist cannot use the splash to write a book about distribution, though he might write one about baking cookies. The response has been overwhelmingly positive. The best plans and the best processes will turn to dust in the hands of untrained, unprepared, uninformed, or unmotivated people.

Each of these vital business operations—Measurement, Management, Motivation; Plan, Process, and People—is important in its own right. And, when driven by an intelligent attitude toward managing risk, the benefits are synergistic and cumulative. Better measurement produces better planning, which makes it possible to manage processes more efficiently, and so forth. The more you "do" them, the more proficient you become. Individually and collectively, successful practice is driven by attitude, by an innovative new product mindset that leads managers and teams to produce newness in the marketplace.

In Summary

This book is devoted to creating the kind of risk-embracing new product culture of innovation that has been the source of real long-term growth for most companies. Risk is inevitable, but so is increased growth and profitability for those who have the courage to persist and persevere.

CHAPTER 2

The Seven Components of the MAP™ System

*D*on't be afraid to fail

You've failed many times, although you may not remember. You fell down the first time you tried to walk. You almost drowned the first time you tried to swim, didn't you? Did you hit the ball the first time you swung a bat? Heavy hitters, the ones who hit the most home runs, also strike out a lot.

R. H. Macy failed seven times before his store in New York caught on. English novelist John Creasy got 753 rejection slips before he published 564 books. Babe Ruth struck out 1,330 times, but he also hit 714 home runs. Don't worry about failure. Worry about chances you miss when you don't even try.

United Technologies Corporation 1986

Companies first beginning to consciously develop new products often find themselves in a sea of confusion. There are lots of ideas, some with potential, others not. Different team members have different interests and different levels of enthusiasm. And of course there are the costs, both potential and actual. The number of missed opportunities and misaligned resources can be considerable. As with any new activity, a guide—or a MAP—can be invaluable.

On one hand, the notion of a MAP is a new approach to new product innovation. On the other hand, it is as old as new products themselves. It draws together and organizes a company's skill and assets to their greatest effect. Then, driven by the right attitude toward risk, the chances for success are maximized.

Risk is the Backbone

In the simplest terms, risk can be defined as the probability of success or failure. It is the backbone of new product development. It is the central core, the spinal cord, the brainstem. Companies are in the business of reducing risk and maximizing returns. But it is easy to forget that both need to be in balance. And both need to exist. Without risk, there is little potential reward. On the other hand, return potential drives management to develop and launch new products, but an aversion to risk impedes it from doing so. Ask yourself how many new product concepts have been killed not by the results of careful analysis or research but because of management's fear of risk.

Don't be misled into believing that companies take a less creative approach to new products if they build upon their existing strengths. There are limited capital and human resources in any company. Structuring new product innovation enables a company to optimize these two scarce resources rather than minimize and dilute their impact. As a result, those limited resources are utilized in ways that will decrease risk and increase payback. Building innovation should be a predictable and manageable endeavor—not a dice game dependent on luck.

So what can management do? First, companies need to strike a better balance between the uphill battle for consistent quarterly earnings and the longer-term return expected from investments in high-risk categories. At present, management's focus on near-term profitability is its major obstacle to new product success. Second, management needs to create a corporate environment that encourages risk taking and reinforces an entrepreneurial attitude. Third, it needs to establish realistic criteria for success. Success in new products requires a different set of metrics than those used for established or emerging businesses. Key metric areas to consider for new products include:

- ✧ Ensure that new products and services are satisfying *strategic objectives.*
- ✧ Create an ongoing *pipeline* of new products at each step of the development process.
- ✧ Develop a *portfolio* consisting of different risk and return types for new products and services.
- ✧ Generate a higher *Return on Innovation Investment* from one year to the next.
- ✧ Achieve a *success rate of 50 percent* or better on all commercialized new products.

In this way, companies will be better able to see a business's new product development function as a discipline that requires ongoing resources, organizational support, and funding. It's not just an opportunity that gets pursued sporadically. The key to success is to understand how best to deal with, rather than to ignore, the risk inherent in any new product development.

Successful companies start by first understanding their internal strengths and weaknesses to establish clearly which pillars to build upon in developing new products. The chances for failure grow exponentially as a company introduces a product that doesn't play off its existing strengths. This does not mean that companies should develop only lots of line extensions and additions that are nothing more than feature or flavor changes to existing products. Rather, it implies that to some extent the existing competitive advantages of a company should be exploited when developing a new product. Brand-name equity, a low-cost manufacturing process, proprietary technology, channel clout, and category market-share leadership all represent examples of strengths upon which new products can draw. Yet many companies go after new products that have no relationship to their existing strengths. That doesn't mean that they are doomed to certain failure, but this approach always increases the risk.

Consequently, management must be able to accept uncertainty and cope with risk. New product failures are unavoidable. They are a part of the success formula. The key is for management to recognize and feel reasonably comfortable that certain approaches can help to diminish the risk, even though they can never eliminate it.

The Seven Elements of New Product Innovation

Innovation is not a creative, unstructured brainstorming activity. It is a multifunctional and disciplined management process that fuses analysis with creativity. Most companies cannot afford the luxury of sitting around a conference table to "blue sky" hundreds of ideas and, in turn, funnel them though a costly screening and development process. Rather, a focus on customer needs and company-specific new product objectives and growth roles that new products are intended to satisfy should focus idea generation and concept development.

Companies also need to encourage managers to use their intuition, rather than to conserve it. Call it business judgment or gut feel if you wish. The key is to make managers realize that blending business analysis and knowledge with intuition and creativity will bolster success.

During the past two and one-half decades, I've looked at and worked with many successful innovation companies. The *best* tended to have a certain set of skills, tools, and mindsets that their competition didn't have. The *best* had a continuous stream of new products and services. It's as if the *best* had

EXHIBIT 2.1 The New Product MAP™ System

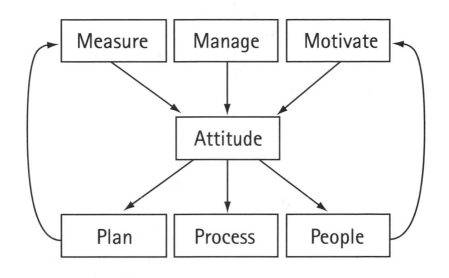

somehow figured out how to build a new products "factory." In fact, they had.

Innovation can be managed and systematically executed. The rest of the book spells out this system for new product development—the New Product MAP™ System—depicted in Exhibit 2.1.

I call it MAP because management needs a map that offers guidelines for everyone to use and shows which direction to turn.

The letters M, A, and P depict the seven key components of the MAP™ System.

This system is actually very easy to put in place once management believes that all seven pieces are required to ignite innovation systematically and in a way that drives growth. There are three skills: measure, manage, and motivate; and there are three tools: plan, process, and people. In the middle, between the skills and tools, is attitude or mindset, which is the linchpin for the entire system. Attitude is the glue that holds it all together. The system focuses on measuring the plan, managing the process, and motivating the people. Uniting these activities is a risk-taking, team-oriented, spirited attitude.

The book is organized around these components to provide you with practical hands-on descriptions of how to set up the MAP™ System within your own company. Your goal should be to figure out how best to persuade your management that the MAP™ System will dramatically improve your company's track record in new product and service development.

Measure

Everything is relative. Success is little more than an opinion if you cannot compare it to something else. Being able to monitor your growth allows you to learn from past successes and failures.

New product analysts need to regularly monitor the performance of new products in order to compare the actual results with the original forecasts. They need to identify the variance in performance needs and uncover the causal factors that influence a new product's performance. The primary purpose of a formalized tracking system is to identify development costs, new product performance relative to original objectives, and competitive responses after launch. The major benefits of a tracking system are to establish a database that improves future forecasting and to develop a rationale for each new product's success or failure. Such a system also offers insights into ways to change future new products and provides a mechanism to monitor overall performance when managing new products.

Top management and new product management need a report card that defines how well the process is working and how new products have performed. Often, once they launch a new product, it becomes part of the annual budget of an existing business. However, the business must examine the new product's financial projections relative to the original forecasts. Another part of documenting new product performance is to track the competitive response to a launch. Competitors' retaliatory actions against a new product frequently will affect the original forecasts negatively, but management must know how much competition affected performance to correct for unrealistic assumptions.

Moreover, carefully tracking development costs is needed to determine the overall payoff of the new product program. You must calculate more than just invested capital. You must integrate the labor costs and research time that were allocated into the new product budgets. There should be a separate budget established for all related new product development costs. Of course, a separate budget means that management will be able to clearly identify whether the investment is generating an adequate return. Hiding new product failures under the carpet only perpetuates a risk-averse, me-too approach to new products. Thus, tracking new product performance is a key step in identifying a company's internal strengths and weaknesses. And that identification is an underlying principle in successful new product development.

Manage

The more successful companies specify who is accountable for attaining new products results. One person is usually responsible for managing the entire new product process in any successful new product organization. Obviously, the president of a division, sector, group, or company is ultimately responsible for having successful new products meet the financial goals established. But who is accountable on a daily basis for managing new product concepts through the process to commercialization? Who recommends moving the priority of one product ahead of another? Who organizes the market research? Who mediates between manufacturing and research and development when they disagree? Who explains to top management why the development of a project is taking longer than anticipated? Who recommends how to allocate resources efficiently?

A committee, team, or multidisciplinary task force cannot do these activities without a leader. A team is indeed most appropriate to use in marshaling requisite resources to develop new products, but one person needs to be accountable for operation of the process. It should be someone who has no existing business crises to attend to and does not have conflicts of interest such as budget allocation or personnel hiring. This person should be directly responsible for the day-to-day activities involved with developing new products, and his/her compensation at the end of the year will be decidedly affected by new product performance.

It should be someone who cannot easily evade responsibility. Most important, this person oversees the progress of all phases of the new product development function, from market research to idea generation to prototype development and testing, to outcomes. Titles range from new product manager or director of innovation to vice-president of diversification or director of new-business expansion.

Motivate

Finding ways to build personal self-esteem is the key to motivating people. Once employees feel valued, they will feel more confident and, in turn, will be successful innovators.

Most companies will buy into all aspects of formalizing new product development except for the one major and common missing link—motivation and rewards. This is a mistake. Compensation and financial incentives are integral ingredients of the motivation and reward game plan. Although dollars and cents are not the only means of motivating a team of new product developers, money does talk, and companies that want an entrepreneurial environment need to have compensation programs that simulate those of a start-up business. Unfortunately, most large companies relentlessly resist any changes in compensation practices.

If you want people to act like risk-taking entrepreneurs, then treat them that way. Provide enough economic incentive so new product team members are willing to commit themselves to getting successful new products out the door. Make the incentive contingent upon the actual performance of new products in the marketplace. If the product fizzles out, then the bonus is $0. On the other hand, if a new product adds $1 million in profits, then why shouldn't the new product manager receive a $50,000 bonus?

The key is tying some portion of compensation to the new

product's performance. Whatever the benchmarks or rewards are, something different is needed to stimulate, motivate, and reinforce risk-taking on the part of new product development managers.

Psychological, emotional, and career advancement awards are also powerful motivators. It doesn't cost a nickel to create a positive atmosphere. People know when their judgments are valued. A workplace that emphasizes mutual respect and co-operation becomes self-motivating.

Attitude

Creating an attitude that embraces risk-taking and innovation gives people permission to pursue truly new products and services. A mindset that supports the costs and time required to develop new products must be pervasive throughout the organization.

Ultimately, top management either makes or breaks the success of new product development programs. Commitment to new products comes from the top. Without it, even the most creative, dynamic, and gung-ho manager will most likely fail in commercializing new products successfully. So the first message that top management must communicate throughout a company is that they have a high degree of commitment to internally developed new products and consider them to be critical to growth. All levels of management across functional and operating divisions must understand and believe in the role of new products within a company.

Top management must demonstrate commitment—not just talk about the need for it. Commitment can be demonstrated by assigning the best managers to new products, by rewarding new product participants with incentives consistent with long-term goals, by treating new products as an investment center rather than an expense, and by providing leadership that pulls all functional managers together in backing the new product effort.

The following are other tangible signs of top management commitment to new products:

- ✧ Having lunch monthly with the new products group.
- ✧ Speaking a common new products language that cross-functional people understand.
- ✧ Visiting the laboratory and wearing a white coat for a day.
- ✧ Attending a new product focus group to hear problems and needs communicated by customers.
- ✧ Writing personal memos to new product personnel—to people directly and indirectly involved in the process—commending their contributions.
- ✧ Holding an annual awards dinner that rewards the top five new product teams in the company.

The point is that beyond consistently providing the people and funds needed to manage new products, top management must act in ways that illustrate to managers an interest, involvement, and willingness to participate in the process. And not only does this demonstration of top management commitment signal the importance of new products, it also generates tangible rewards that link directly back to our discussion of motivation and rewards.

Making a commitment to growth through internally developed new products calls for a proactive attitude on the part of top management. The less confident and risk-averse executive may be far more willing to spend capital and allocate human resources to ongoing businesses than on unfamiliar and unproven new product ventures. The key is getting top management to board the tumultuous new product roller coaster and hang on for the ride.

Plan

You cannot get anything accomplished without a plan that describes the roles new products are to serve and the agreed-upon expectations about how well they should perform. Although there is the occasional serendipitous winner, ongoing new product success does not happen by accident.

New Product Blueprint. The New Product Blueprint describes the role of new products relative to a company's growth objectives and strategy. The blueprint states the intended roles for new products in satisfying the corporate strategy. The risk posture of top management, long-term financial objectives of the corporation, and five-year growth strategy contribute to the blueprint. Companies can reach growth targets by investing in and expanding the existing business (or by acquiring companies), by forming strategic alliances, or by launching internally developed new products. The essential purpose of the new product blueprint is to articulate in writing, and to place dimensions around, the expected role that new products will play in fulfilling corporate growth objectives.

Companies can select, or in some cases their situation may select for them, one of five growth roles to outline their vision for new products. This role will determine the amount of time, money, and human resources needed to dedicate towards new product development in order to achieve its desired results.

The first role is the *Zero Role*, where new products virtually play no role in the future growth of the company.

Next, is the *Upgrade Role*, which concentrates on line extensions, revisions, and additions to existing products. A company that chooses this role chiefly concerns itself with assuring that it has competitively positioned its products and tends to expect new products to contribute less than 10 percent of annual revenues.

A *Modest Growth Role* requires a portfolio of new products that includes new to the world and new to the company along with line extensions and improvements. A modest growth company dedicates a deliberate portion of its portfolio to brand new products, which account for 10 to 20 percent of its annual revenues.

Companies that fall into the *High Growth Role* category have committed themselves to innovative activity and the development of new products as its primary growth mode. This kind of company will also pursue the development of new categories that will allow it to enter totally new businesses. These new products will often contribute more than 20 percent of annual revenues.

Finally, the *Survival Role* is where companies also participate in new product development, but tend to react to competition by only releasing "me-too" products, ones with minor improvements, lower prices, or new bells and whistles. They take a reactionary approach rather than a proactive one.

Any of these new product growth roles may be appropriate for any company at any given time. After all, the roles of new products change over time in most companies. Moreover, there may be a combination of roles within a corporation because different divisions have distinct new product needs and objectives. They often overlook this important fact. Generally, a company's planning cycle occurs every twelve months. External market forces, competition, consumer preferences, and financial requirements can change and consequently alter the role of new products.

The new product manager usually drafts the new product blueprint in concert with top management. The approval process must include senior management in order to build a feeling of involvement and commitment throughout the company. Regardless of the choices, the company must select a role and follow that track. And, everyone in the company must know the role; i.e. the new product manager must distribute the blueprint to everyone involved with new products. This way, no one will be confused about the company's goals.

New Product Strategy and Diagnostic Audit. The New Product Strategy identifies the guidelines: that is, growth gap, strategic roles, and screening criteria for playing the new products game. Companies need to identify how new products will help fill their five-year financial gap and satisfy strategic roles defined in the long-range plan. Should the company be developing new products or focusing on other growth routes (e.g., acquisitions, joint ventures)? What are the roles that new product types will play in the company's overall growth strategy? The development of a new product strategy will reveal the answer to these questions.

Developing a new product strategy serves as management's rudder to steer new product resources along a chartered course. In effect, the strategy helps decide how to best allocate human and financial resources in order to meet the business objectives that the new products would be satisfying. The three key components of a new product strategy are (1) the financial growth gap, (2) strategic roles, and (3) screening criteria. The best way to start this process is by identifying the underlying factors that have contributed to a company's past new product performance. Conducting a self-assessment, or diagnostic audit, on the company's past performance can accomplish this. It is described in Chapter 3.

Companies can determine *the growth gap* after examining how they established goals during previous new products programs. The diagnostic audit provides a perspective on past performance that can be extrapolated into future projections. Given the resources, directions, and funds that supported previous new product efforts, how realistic were the new products goals? Understanding how financial objectives were developed is often valuable when setting new goals. The new product growth gap is the difference between total expected corporate revenues and the forecasted revenues from other growth modes, e.g., acquisitions, joint ventures, and existing business expansion. The growth gap calibrates the total revenues and profits expected during a five-year period that will be generated from new products.

Once the growth gap has been determined, the next task in designing a new product strategy is defining *the strategic roles* that the new products will satisfy. This step is vitally important to success. Without it, revenue and profit generation is the only role that companies will perceive new products to play. While revenue and profit are, of course, the objectives of all new products, that role by itself provides little direction for new product activities. Strategic roles enable managers to see the purpose of a new product beyond financial benefits.

We classify new product strategic roles into two categories:

❖ Requisite roles—describe the functions or expectations that new products are to satisfy in defending, expanding, or bolstering the existing products or services.

❖ Expansive roles—define the ways that new products can propel a company into new categories, markets, or businesses.

Screening criteria should be used to determine the relative attractiveness of each new product concept and category. New product screening criteria must be both qualitative and quantitative. Criteria for qualitative new product screens often include examination of the consumer need, market, risk, strategic role, internal strengths, and competition. In contrast, the quantitative screens may include requirements on minimal revenue thresholds, gross margin minimums, payback periods, returns on capital, or returns on assets for any product that is new to the company. Nevertheless, screens need to reflect the relative degree of risk that differs between new product types and the strategic role they intend to satisfy. As the risk increases from line extension to new-to-the-world products, the expected return needs to be higher to accommodate the risk.

Process

No plan is worth trying to achieve without a proper process. The important part is assuring that the process is understood by everyone and adhered to with rigor and discipline. The cornerstone of any successful endeavor is consistency. The most successful companies have had the same new product development process in place for five years or more. They know how it works and why it yields consistent results.

The process component of the MAP™ System contains ten steps:

1. Needs and Wants Exploration. Before idea generation begins, exploratory market and customer research is an essential component of the new product development process. This vital stage provides the foundation and platform for effective idea generation. It describes customer or consumer needs, wants, gripes, complaints, and problems that each have about the performance of a certain activity, function, process, life event, or product. This research, prior to idea generation, provides the basis for setting up a problem-solving mindset towards idea generation.

2. Idea Generation. Now is the time to begin the creative, brainstorming, and association-making process of developing new ideas. Companies can utilize a wide variety of approaches to generate new product ideas. New ideas hardly ever seem to be lacking in companies. There are, however, a number of tools and approaches that can be used to solicit ideas:

- One-on-one interviews or group sessions
- Patent searches
- Warranty cards
- Questionnaires and surveys
- Trade shows
- Trips to foreign countries
- Purchased and customized consumer research
- Focus groups

3. Concept Development. Turning an idea into a concept means giving the idea form, substance, and shape—making a rough sketch, giving it a price range and name. The concept must describe the real, functional, or perceived benefits of the new product concept. The task is to apply screening criteria *loosely* to each concept. Loosely is the appropriate word. New product teams should complete all the in-depth screening later in the process. That then becomes the database to screen out or in specific new product concepts. *Note: Some initial screening takes place here to determine which concepts warrant business analysis. Keep in mind that some screens, those aligned with strategic role or new product type, have already been conducted, and that many screens are still to come in the screening part of the process.*

4. Business Analysis. Business analysis of a new product concept requires examining the dynamics of the category, competition, cost positions, and consumer buying patterns, and matching them with internal strengths in order to develop financial projections. Specific components of business analysis should include the following:

- Market trends and growth potential
- Competition
- Complementary product performance
- Barriers and costs to enter and serve the market
- Product unit costs
- Financial projections

5. Screening. Once a company has conducted the business analysis for a concept, managers should then pass it through the financial screens that the new product strategy has established. This is often a good point at which to receive management approval for prototype development.

6. Prototype development. Companies very often have developed a sample or some other type of prototype by this stage in the process. But now is the time to design the new service or product and identify the cost of materials and manufacturing or systems costs, etc. Moreover, manufacturing, customer service, and information technology and systems support must now be actively involved with the research lab or engineering staff. Companies waste a lot of time when teams hand a product to manufacturing that won't work outside of the lab. The objective at this stage of a new product's development is to get one or more prototypes that are in final form for consumer testing, are cost determinable, and are able to be made or delivered. New product managers must remain involved—they cannot just turn the project over to the technicians.

7. Market Testing. Companies often forget this stage. Excitement, anticipation, competitive threats, and management emotion creep into the minds of managers. They have now developed a product that passes the screens, and management already perceives the product to be a winner. The goal is to make sure that it is indeed a winner and to make the product even better. The objective of a test market is to determine whether a new product will fly and if developers need to make changes prior to launch. However, the main advantage is to provide real-life direction on how to improve the positioning, packaging, pricing, and advertising. By doing this step, a company reduces the risk of failure during commercialization.

While test markets do take time and money, companies need to ask themselves if they can afford *not* to perform these market tests.

8. Plant Scale-up. At this point, someone must make the decision to launch the product or not. The company may need to purchase additional equipment, shift factory lines, or add new tooling. The plant also needs to test the product in large enough quantities to ensure product quality.

9. Commercialization. Timing, coordination and carefully planned execution and communication are the cornerstones of a successful launch. Once the new product team has proven that the test results are adequate and made the decision to go forward, they must bring the sales force up to speed and properly motivate them to garner their commitment behind the product. Often companies neglect this important step. They must "sell it" to the sales force just as they must persuade the consumer to buy. Moreover, the execution of the launch must be properly timed, adequately supported, and closely monitored to make adjustments to the initial program. Identification of the target customer, product positioning, and competitive advantage must be factored into the development of the rollout plan. The underlying cause behind many product failures is poor execution during this phase of the process. A new product may still be further refined during the first six to nine months in the marketplace.

10. *Postlaunch Checkup.* Companies often overlook this step which can provide significant leverage in the development of successful new products. Management frequently revises forecasts once the new product has been in the marketplace for six months. Financial management forgets the original estimates, and by year two no one in the organization has any recollection of what they were, never mind measuring performance against them. Remembering to monitor performance throughout the six and twelve months following launch relative to the original forecasts is crucial. After one year, re-evaluate performance annually.

People

We have not yet innovated enough to let computers make all of our decisions for us. That is why the People component is actually the ignition for starting the entire MAP™ System. Teamwork, communications, tenure, and experience are key factors for ensuring that people will innovate effectively.

Teamwork and Communication. Teamwork requires a leader; effective communication requires frequent dialogue. One way companies can foster teamwork is by having a leader in place who provides an environment where open communication is the norm. New products do not allow people to work independently for a month, then regroup, and report on progress. At a minimum, weekly dialogue among the key new product players is a must. One way to solidify a leadership position for the team is by having a full-time person assigned to manage the process.

When they expect new products to play an important role in the organization, responsible new product management must report directly to the top. The new product effort demands top management visibility and exposure. Elevating the position and status of the new product manager signals several things to employees:

- ✧ New products are as important to the organization as the other functional and operational entities.
- ✧ Top management is committed to, and involved with, new products.
- ✧ The new product effort has a clearly defined leader and a group of dedicated resources.
- ✧ New product development is an ongoing function of the organization and not an ad hoc task force or temporary committee.

In addition, as a sign of commitment, management should consider budgeting for new products in concert with existing business investments rather than subordinate to them.

For those of you who do not have the new product organization reporting directly to top management, a rationale may exist. But change it tomorrow. Identify a person who can be held accountable for new products. Whatever it takes—get the new product function reporting to the top decision-making layer of management within the organization.

In short, establishing a separate new product organization with one person who reports to top management clearly accountable for new products will greatly enhance the probabilities of new product success and significantly improve communications. Moreover, instilling a sense of teamwork and establishing formal communication mechanisms are integral parts of the success formula. Part IV will contain more about the building of the organization.

Tenure and Experience. A myth that continues to permeate most of corporate America is that one cannot have a career in new products. However, some smart companies are recognizing the tremendous advantage that comes with having veterans on the new product team. The reason is that accumulated experience does breed success. As a result, not only do the crafty veterans create the means for a successful program, but also the new people that come to the new product area have trained mentors who can expedite the learning process for them.

Successful companies understand the benefits and value of tenure. Longevity in the new product area usually leads to a seasoned understanding of how the process works. Moreover, product champions do not spring up overnight. A person needs time working with new products to feel comfortable with the process before emotionally committing to and standing behind a concept. Enlightened companies have fully dedicated new product people, who receive bonuses, vacations, and promotions—just like other business managers.

Constantly infusing new people into the new product process is not the key to creativity. If anything, churning managers through this complex management process stifles creativity. How can you be creative unless you know what you are doing? It is far better to develop and nurture a group of managers who have been through the wringer, understand how new products are developed, and maintain a consistent and systematic approach. Consistency breeds creativity and effective results. It is the attitude and energy level underlying the experience base that breeds success.

An architect who has been designing houses for years can often design a creative and unique house. Brand new architects are not the creative masters of this art form—the veterans are. Likewise, the contractor who has a cadre of experienced and skilled workers building the house will perform a better job of constructing the house than the newly opened construction shop will. You can compare the new product strategy to the building's blueprint, the new product team to the seasoned construction company, the new product manager to the head architect and job foreman.

Management has to deal with new product people differently if they desire successful results. This is by no means meant to imply that new product managers should be given free rein to do their own thing. It does suggest that the motivation factors, compensation, and incentive structures, in concert with the managerial style, must be different from those of managers of existing businesses. The question therefore becomes how to put people into a structured analytical process who are encouraged to think and act in ways that build personal value, self-esteem, and team effectiveness.

In Summary

When it comes down to the basics, the same components are constant for everyone. From the newest computer company, to the largest car manufacturer, to the smallest service provider, the MAP™ outlines exactly what needs to be done to improve your success in new product generation. If there is one lesson to be learned, it is this: no company—regardless of size of budget, stock price, employee base, or number of existing products—is exempt from any of the MAP™ System components.

The most important thing about these components is that none of them could be omitted without increasing the rate of failure. Could you imagine producing a product without a plan, without commitment from the employees, without proper management, without *people*! Of course you couldn't. So draw out the map, make copies and hand it out all around your company.

The Plan

The most important part of virtually any activity is the plan. Without a solid new product plan, it is impossible to know where you are going, how you will get there, and whether or not you have succeeded. This part of the book is devoted to the three key parts of every new product plan: the diagnostic audit, the new product blueprint, and the new product strategy. The audit is probably the most important *and* most overlooked *and* most abused part of the planning process. It is vitally important because it tells the planner where the company's new products "have been," which is essential to setting a course for the future. From the audit come the new product blueprint, which outlines the parameters of the program and the strategy, which sets the specific course.

CHAPTER 3

The Diagnostic Audit

- *The "best" new product companies tend to have higher stock prices than their competitors more often than the "rest."*
- *The "best" new product companies recognize the contribution of new product and service development to their stock price more often than the "rest."*
- *The "best" new product companies tend to be more profitable than the "rest."*
- *The "best" new product companies tend to be market "innovators" while the "rest" tend to be "risk-averse."*

From: "Winning New Products and Service Practices." Kuczmarski & Associates/Kellogg Graduate School of Management. Oct. 1999.

The old belief that people are often destroyed by their successes and saved by the lessons learned from their failures certainly applies to new product development. The diagnostic audit targets both of those events, making it possible to capitalize on things done right and to avoid those that weren't. The audit pinpoints what to fix from the past and how to develop the blueprint for the future. It is the tool a company can use to identify internal assets and weaknesses in order to develop a more robust new product blueprint and strategy.

In short, the new product diagnostic audit directs the development of a new product strategy that should enable a company to optimize its allocation of resources, match its new product activities to growth objectives, and focus management attention on the key areas of new product development for the company. The audit will pinpoint areas where changes can be made to improve the success rate of commercialized new products. Understanding the past will yield better results in the future.

Developing new products is a focused, multidisciplinary process that fuses external market needs with internal functional capabilities. The first challenge is to identify the internal equities and sources of competitive advantage that can be used to make a new product unique and sustainable. These two challenges mean that information is critical. That's why the toughest part of conducting a diagnostic audit is developing an approach for gathering and analyzing the data needed to evaluate a company's new product performance. Companies' needs, resources, and cultures differ, but the four-part approach shown in this chapter is useful for all companies.

How to Conduct the Audit

This chapter will describe each part of the audit in detail. Following are the four parts of a new product diagnostic audit:

1. *Historical new product performance* examines the past new product performance for the overall company or the division as well as for each commercialized new product.

2. *Strengths-and-weaknesses assessment* analyzes the internal functional strengths and weaknesses and identifies the major leverage points upon which to build a new product strategy and focus consumer research.

3. *Best-practice scoreboard* compares a company's new product practice to the competition's and to the success formula of other "winning" new product companies.

4. *Top management commitment* evaluates the degree of top management commitment to the new product effort.

For the most part, historical new product performance is the key "roll up" category because it defines the overall success or failure of a company's new products effort. If the historical record reflects unsuccessful performance, the reason can inevitably be found in the company's strengths and weaknesses, the presence or absence of best practices, or the degree of management commitment. These three parts of an audit reflect the efficiency and effectiveness of a company's new products program. Given the comprehensive coverage represented in the historical performance category, it isn't surprising to assume that you most likely will spend approximately 50 percent of your time on that exercise and split the remainder evenly among the other three parts. This is not to imply that the other three categories aren't as important. Rather, as mentioned previously, they tend to be reflected in the historical category.

Company and Project Data Needs

New product-related data must be collected and analyzed at two levels: performance at the individual product level and performance at the overall company or division level. Historical new product information often migrates to the dark corners of corporate inactive files. By interviewing management and digging through old files and surveys, however, it is possible to reconstruct a fairly clear picture. Interviews—especially with former new product people—can be invaluable, but it is important to be sensitive to the egos that may still be vulnerable, especially if the product was a bomb. Interviewees may be defensive if the product failed badly.

Getting Started

Once senior management has bought into the process of conducting a diagnostic audit, the first step is developing a preliminary plan of action to cover all four parts of the diagnostic audit. Two actions are helpful:

1. Gather all internal documents on new products, including strategic plans, new product portfolios, technology plans, product business plans, and approval documents, to understand the status of existing data and projects.
2. Identify 10 representative new product projects (5 successes and 5 failures) that will be examined in depth to identify the lessons (both pro and con) to be learned and applied to the process going forward.

EXHIBIT 3.1 Minidiagnostic Audit Checklist

These questions can serve as a mini-audit—as a backdrop against which key topics can be focused. The answers to these questions should provide a snapshot of some of the challenges facing your company in the new product arena and indicate how badly the company needs a full audit.

✧ What have been the major internal factors influencing the company's new product performance during the past three to five years?

✧ What new products have competitors introduced within the past five years? How have their new products performed in comparison to yours? Why?

✧ Which current functional strengths have had the greatest and most frequent impact on successfully commercialized new products?

✧ What specific shortfalls should you correct in the following areas?

- Sales and marketing

- Manufacturing

- Research and development

- Engineering

- Finance

- Market research

✧ What strategic roles have new products satisfied for the company, and how has performance contributed to the company's financial objectives?

✧ On what types of new products has the company focused, for example, totally new to the world, new lines to the company, line extensions and adaptations, new additions to existing lines, cost reductions?

✧ What screening criteria have been used to evaluate new products that have been under development? Under what circumstances did the criteria change?

✧ How effective are the communication and coordination between the sales/marketing, manufacturing, and engineering functions? How does the current process address the need for multidisciplinary integration in the development process?

✧ What formal and informal communication mechanisms foster team interaction in the development process?

✧ How does the current organization structure enhance the management of the new product process?

✧ What are the major weaknesses?

✦ How can the current process, approval procedures, and development time be streamlined to decrease the gestation time of new products?

✦ Who does the company hold accountable for new products, and who measures the performance of new product managers? Where in the organization should the new product effort report?

✦ What types of compensation incentives or reward systems does the company use to support the objectives, structure, and process?

✦ What role has top management played in the new product program?

In answering these questions, a company will begin to understand some of the reasons for its new product performance. The answers, moreover, will indicate the types of objectives and roles that new products will play in meeting the overall growth objectives of the company. Now a company is ready to take a deeper look at its past products and seek out key lessons learned to carry forward into tomorrow's new product program.

Gathering Qualitative and Quantitative Data

Once schedules for the audit have been set, meet with a group of multifunctional managers involved in new products, and generate a chronological list of product launches, determining new product types for each product. If the company undergoing the diagnostic audit has an extensive history in new products, then have the group limit its analysis to the ten representative projects already selected. Otherwise, it will take months to complete the audit.

At this point, it is important to enlist the help of a finance person who can begin downloading company new product performance records. These records should include revenues, profits, and budgets as well as individual project costs, forecasts, revenues, and profits. Once the groundwork is completed, the diagnostic audit can begin.

Start at the company level by interviewing key upper management and new product participants. Get their views of the key success factors for product development, internal strengths and weaknesses compared to the competition, and any issues related to communications, development process, performance measurement, or organizational issues. It is then important to interview or survey all other new product managers until a clear picture of the company's situation emerges. You will find examples of questionnaires for best practices, strengths-and-weaknesses assessment, and top-management commitment later in this chapter.

With this overview of the key new product issues facing the company, you can now turn to the product data, which provides specific additional support for broader company-level observations. Start by interviewing product or project managers, current and past, to get their insights and their perceptions of products they were involved with. If the company uses multifunctional teams, it is important to interview at least two team members to account for any biased perceptions.

At the product level, one must determine the following key features of each product:

1. Identify the project rationale.
2. Create a project time line that includes key milestones and key events (i.e., technical hurdles, changes in the marketplace).
3. Define new product type.
4. Determine the level of risk involved. Obtain project costs, revenues, and returns if the finance person does not have them. Obtain additional project documentation to support verbal estimates and subjective conclusions about the project.

To gain an overall picture, the diagnostic audit should include interviews with direct competitors, companies in related or similar industries, customers, distributors, associations, and industry experts. These interviews will disclose external perceptions of the company's new product performance as well as establish effectiveness and efficiency benchmarks for comparison.

Historical New Product Performance

Part 1 of the diagnostic audit evaluates the company's new product track record. It looks at the financial and strategic performance of the company's total new product portfolio as well as each new product introduced during the previous five years (or longer depending on the company's product life cycle and average development time). Beyond examining the company's new product record, it also looks at the development process, resource allocation mix, and new product activity of competitors.

There are six dimensions to the historical analysis:

1. Identifying historical new product revenue and profit performance.
2. Determining the new product survival rate.
3. Assessing new product performance against original objectives—the success rate.
4. Determining the underlying causes behind new product success or failure.
5. Pinpointing new product development time and costs—the payback.
6. Identifying strengths of top new product competitors.

Identifying Historical New Product Revenue and Profit Performance

Each step of the Historical New Product Performance adds insight into the company's new product strengths. Begin with the historical revenue—*identify the historical revenue and profit performance*—by listing new products by year of introduction. Second, categorize each new product according to one of the following seven new product types:

1. New to the world/new to the country. Products that create a totally new category or market. (imac by Apple, the Balance Bar, and DVD by Sony)
2. New to the company. Products that may already exist in one form or another but not in your company. (Lincoln Navigator, Virgin Cola, and Avandia—a diabetes drug)
3. Line extension/flanker. Products that are closely related to an existing line and provide a way to expand

the number of products offered to customers, for example, new flavors, new sizes. (Vlasic Hamburger
Stackers, Frosted Cheerios)

4. Revision or improvement to an existing product line.
   Products that offer improved performance or greater
   price/value to customers. These frequently replace an
   existing line item. (Continental Lite airline service,
   and American Express Blue Card)

5. Cost reduction. Products that have a lower manufacturing unit cost than formerly. Consumers may or may
   not perceive these as also having a product improvement. (Sprint and AT&T long-distance service)

6. Repositioning. Existing products that companies re-
   formulate, repackage, or send back to the market to attract new customers or pursue a new market.
   (Volkswagen New Beetle)

7. Licensed, joint ventured, or acquired new products.
   New products that companies generate through licensing agreements, a majority or minority joint venture with another company, or products that they
   acquire from another company. (P&G acquired Iams
   pet food products)

Generally, there are three ways to define new product types regardless of company or industry. Exhibit 3.2 ranks new product types by level of technology newness, perceived newness
by the market, and newness to the company. You should consider all three criteria when defining a new product type. For
example, a biotechnology company may be more concerned
with newness in terms of technology, and a consumer products
company may be more interested in newness in terms of the
market. Neither company, however, should focus exclusively
on one or the other, because they need to translate newness according to industry, company, and market maturation. The ex-

EXHIBIT 3.2 Defining New Product Types

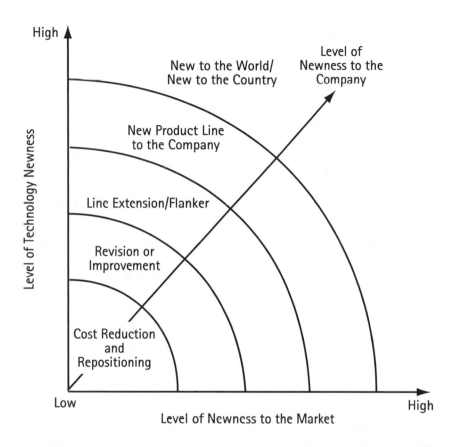

 amples in Exhibit 3.3 illustrate how companies can define new products by type.

Three more new innovations along with their results are depicted in Exhibit 3.4. The next steps are to calculate annual and cumulative revenues and profits for each product during the past five years. List annual revenues and profits by year for each product and add them up to determine cumulative revenues and profits during the time period.

EXHIBIT 3.3 New Product Types

NEW TO THE WORLD/NEW TO THE COUNTRY

New to the world in second edition
Disposable camera

In late 1987 the Japanese film giant Fuji introduced its Fuji Color Quick Snap disposable camera in Japan. After its initial success, Fuji went global. Eastman Kodak responded with its own disposable, the Fling 35, to compete in this niche market. Combined, Fuji and Kodak sold twenty-one million disposable cameras in Asia and the U.S. in 1988. Recent improvements to the product are an underwater camera and one with a telephoto lens.

The disposable camera, which has the lens attached to the film rather than the film housed in the camera, conveniently offers consumers quality photography when they want to leave their expensive cameras at home or when they forget to bring them.

Where are they now?

The disposable camera continues to be a major player in the film market, despite strong challenges from the Advanced Photo System and digital cameras. Polaroid recently announced its entry into the market by developing the first disposable instant camera, the Popshots camera. In 1999, Kodak received the Gold Medal from the World Environment Center for their recycling efforts with their disposable units. Kodak claims that disposable cameras continue to be a hot product and despite a 7% drop in sales in the first quarter of 1998, traditional—i.e. not disposable—film experienced a 20% drop, which shows great popularity in the disposable market.

New to the world 1999
Digital VCR

It is actually not a VCR at all, but a DVR (Digital Video Recorder). Philips launched its Personal TV project in March 1999, and Replay Networks launched Replay TV in April. These will allow viewers to record numerous hours of television without a videocassette. It is also quite interactive in terms of searching for programming. But the best feature is the ability to pause a program that you are watching—for instance to take a telephone call—and then continue watching from that point at any time, even if the program hasn't ended yet.

Philips' system requires purchasing a processing box for the home and subscribing to the Tivo Personal Television service. Replay Networks' service is free, although the box is more expensive. Both can be used with either cable or antenna feed. Plans to work with DirecTV satellite broadcasting are in the works.

NEW TO THE COMPANY

New to the company in second edition
AT&T Universal Card

AT&T chose the 1990 Academy Awards telecast to launch its newest blockbuster, the Universal Card. The card was AT&T's first attempt to enter the credit-card market. In order to establish itself immediately as a strong player, AT&T offered a lifetime waiver of annual fees to all first-year card applicants. The card was able to achieve 4.1 million accounts in just eight months.

The Universal Card combines the AT&T calling card and a credit card so you only need to carry one card. In addition to providing all Visa and Master Card benefits, Universal gives a 10 percent discount on all AT&T calls charged to the card.

Where are they now?

In 1998 AT&T sold its credit card businesses to Citibank. At that time, it had generated 13.6 million accounts in the United States during its past eight years.

New to the company in 1999
Compaq Aero 2100

Compaq jumped into the very trendy personal digital assistant (PDA) market in early 1999 with a full-color interface. The Microsoft Windows CE operating system also allows for smooth interaction with any Microsoft PC. Compaq is going up against PDA giant 3Com, which holds a 78% stranglehold on the market. The Aero was originally their mini-laptop line, but transferred the name to the PDA.

LINE EXTENSION/FLANKER

Line extension in second edition
Lifesaver Holes

In 1990 Planters introduced the missing piece to longtime favorite Lifesaver candy. Planters leveraged the powerful and well-known Lifesaver name in bringing Lifesaver Holes to the market. The new Holes gained 16 percent of all hard-candy sales in its test market, thus proving the power of brand equity. Planters expect the new candy to overtake Tic-Tac and Certs Mini Mints to become the best-selling bite-size candy.

Where are they now?

Planters has since discontinued the holes line, partly because of the inability to take any of the market from Certs or Tic-Tac and partly because of the negative image created when they had to pull the product off the shelves at one point to re-design the packaging. Several teen-agers had accidentally swallowed—or gagged on—the original containers' plastic flip top. They have realized much more success from their Gummy Savers line, a chewy version of the original round hard candy.

Line extension in 1998
Frito-Lay Wow Chips

Launched in 1998, Wow Chips are the low-fat equivalent of Frito-Lay's traditional snack foods. Riding on the popularity of the FDA approval of Olestra, a cooking oil substitute, Wow generated $347 million in sales in 1998, and was the number-one new product according to Information Resources Inc.

REVISION OR IMPROVEMENT

Revision in second edition
Wide-body tennis racquet

In 1988 Wilson introduced the first innovation in tennis racquet design since the oversize racquet over a decade earlier. Wilson's Profile tennis racquet has a $1/2$-inch thick frame, nearly twice the thickness of conventional racquets, hence the "wide-body" name. With close to $25 million in first-year sales, Wilson's Profile established a permanent position for wide bodies in the racquet market.

The Profile's hollow frame makes the racquet stronger but lightweight, providing the player with more power. The wide body also absorbs greater shock, thereby lessening the chance of tennis elbow, a common player ailment.

Where are they now?

The Profile line evolved into the Hammer line in the early 1990s and has remained that way ever since. It remains as one of the most popular models in the Wilson tennis line—and continues to improve upon itself as tennis technology improves.

Revision in 1999
Intel Pentium III

In March 1999, Intel introduced the newest member of its highly successful Pentium family—the Pentium III microprocessor. With constant demand for faster computers and technology improving every day, the Pentium line is sure to continue to improve upon itself for years to come.

The most important number will be the cumulative profit for each. Cumulative calculations are important because management often forgets that the gestation period for a new product does not necessarily correlate with quarterly earnings reports. Thus, you cannot expect profits to be attractive until a new product has reached the growth stage of its life cycle. Obviously, this stage will be different for each new product.

Cumulative profit should be compared to the original start-up and investment costs. Start-up costs include all initial capital outlays, including those not only for plant scale-up but also for such things as testing equipment required in the initial laboratory stages. This review may provide management with some insights for allocating future dollars against those types of investments that have been most fruitful in the past.

Let's look at a company that introduced more than 125 new products during the past five years. While the bulk of the new products launched were line extensions and flankers, each one required financial development and management time. During a five-year period, new products added $11.7 million in incremental revenues to this $110 million company. Management

EXHIBIT 3.4 New Product Results

1. In March of 1993, Intel Corporation, which produces microprocessors, introduced the Pentium chip. It worked faster than any other chip that had been developed at that time. Since then, Intel has launched the Pentium Pro, the Pentium II and the Pentium III, and has continued to be a major player in the computer chip market.

Result. Since the release of the Pentium, the price of their common stock has grown over 800% on the NASDAQ market. Intel was trading at $5.41 in January 1993. It rose to $7.06 by the launch of Pentium. In January of 1999, Intel reached its all time peak at $70.47, over 1300% higher than only six years before. With Intel's great success, and large-scale volume being sold, it stands not only as a weather-vane stock for technologies, but also for the NASDAQ market as a whole.

2. Continental Airlines declared bankruptcy in 1983, only to reopen its gates 56 hours later. Ten years later, they developed a new service that became known as Continental Lite, an intensely fast, inexpensive way of handling the airline business by connecting smaller airports and charging "peanut fares." This not only eliminated overuse of the airline's hubs, but also established a new world order in the airline industry.

Result. Continental's turnaround is considered by many to be one of the most impressive industry stories of the '90s. Continental's revolutionary program has caused numerous copycat programs to be formed by other airlines. In 1998, Forbes magazine named Continental their Most Improved Company of the 1990s. They continue to lead the industry in capacity growth, and they set their own profit records almost quarterly ($150 million in the 3rd quarter of 1998).

3. In a very interesting adventure into the realm of new products, Volkswagen brought back an old product. It had been 19 years since the classic Beetle had been sold in the United States. The people's car was a favorite of college students and hippies for decades. Volkswagen, which had been experiencing poor sales, gambled on the development of the New Beetle, a modern version of the old classic. They also committed $35 million towards a massive advertising campaign to accompany the car's March 1998 release.

Result. Before the Beetle was even made available, many large dealerships had pre-sold their first three months worth of shipments. Car enthusiasts waited hours at car shows just to sit behind the wheel of the newest edition of German-engineered Americana. Volkswagen experienced its best sales months of the decade and finished the year with its best year since 1981, selling 219,679 new cars. In addition to record sales were all-time high prices on the stock market and numerous awards for quality and advertising, the New Volkswagen Beetle won the most respected prize in the industry: 1999 Motor Trend Import Car of the Year.

EXHIBIT 3.5 Annual New Product Revenues and Profits of a $110 Million Company

	Year 1	Year 2	Year 3	Year 4	Year 5	Cumulative
Annual number of new products	26	21	28	22	28	125
Revenues						
1995 new products	$256,000	$595,000	$836,000	$825,000	$626,000	$3,138,000
1996 new products		$164,000	$1,167,000	$1,344,000	$1,255,000	$3,930,000
1997 new products			$ 346,000	$1,008,000	$1,148,000	$2,502,000
1998 new products				$321,000	$841,000	$1,162,000
1999 new products					$1,008,000	$1,008,000
	$256,000	$759,000	$2,349,000	$3,498,000	$4,878,000	$11,740,000
Operating profits						
Annual	$12,500	$44,000	$164,000	$314,000	$390,000	$924,500
Cumulative	$12,500	$56,500	$220,500	$534,500	$924,500	

had set a target of $10 million in revenues and $1 million in operating profit. The revenue target was clearly met, and the profit target fell short by only $75,000. From a financial standpoint, this company obviously made its new product targets. Annual and cumulative revenues and profits are presented in Exhibit 3.5.

The key is to keep this analysis simple. The purpose is to produce a snapshot of total revenues and profits generated from new products.

The next step is to look at the types of new products developed. For this company, 125 products could be categorized accordingly: new-to-the company (35%) and line extensions and flankers (65%). In other words, two-thirds of the new products introduced by this company were line extensions and flankers to existing product lines. One of the primary strategic roles for new products was to defend market-share position against competitive inroads. Another was to gradually increase share of shelf space. Therefore, in this case the large proportion of line extensions and flankers seems appropriate.

Determine the New Product Survival Rate

Determining the success rate of new products is a function of how well they perform in the marketplace and how well they perform relative to the original objectives set for them. The external survival rate and the internal success rate are the next two measures that the audit will examine. This is the "acid test."

How many of the identified new products have already been taken off the marketplace? Determining the survival rate means identifying what percentage of all new products launched during the past five years are (1) still in the market, (2) already discontinued, (3) scheduled for discontinuation.

Determining the survival rate by new product type often reveals some initial indicators, flashing warning signals, and corrective guideposts for future new product planning. For example, if all the discontinued products are new to the company, perhaps there was not enough testing done in areas in which the company had little understanding or in which requirements to compete were so foreign that it was easier to disregard early signals. Knowing what has actually gone on in the past is the best database for building up the number of successes in the future.

With the product lines new to the company, the company apparently just surveyed the key growth categories and attempted to develop "knockoffs" of competitors' products, doing just a slightly better product than was already on the market. Since distribution channels were unfamiliar to the company, the stage for failure was set. The risk was significantly higher because the company is not building on internal strengths but, rather, trying to capitalize on others' strengths as reflected in a high-growth category.

Based merely on the number of new products launched, it appears that line extensions and cost reductions have been their key survivors in the marketplace. However, until we know the revenue size and profitability of the remaining new-to-the-world and new-to-the-company products, it is difficult to fill in the grade on the report card.

Assessing New Product Performance
Against Original Objectives

Now the internal test begins. How successful have new products been? How realistic are the goals originally set for each new product? Is the company consistently overestimating financial return targets only to get the capital approved to go forward? Are the goals determined according to one single across-the-board hurdle rate? Have the criteria for success been set according to the relative risk/return potential of the new product? How accurate are the forecasts?

The key question then is: How do we define success for new products? Success criteria include: financial performance, the ability to meet strategic objectives, total number of products launched in a year, the quality of new products in the market, time to market, and how well resources for new product development are managed.

The first challenge is to determine the original financial and strategic objectives that were set for the new product. The question, What's our success rate in new products?, can be answered along a number of parameters. Let's examine how closely actual financials resemble original forecasts. Take, for example, a $1 billion corporation that has launched three new products during the past three years. If those three new products generated $6.5 million versus forecast of $22 million in revenues and dropped only $513,000 in profits versus $2,500,000 projected, the judgment is easy: the program is a financial failure.

But there is the strategic dimension. These are the strategic objectives that were developed for the new product program as well as for each new product launched.

- ✧ Overall strategic role for new products: Defend market share position from competitive inroads by foreign competition.
- ✧ Product A: Preempt foreign competition by entering an emerging category segment.
- ✧ Product B: Launch a price-competitive line extension that will increase total line market

      share and deter competition from gaining
      access to distribution channels.

    ✧ Product C: Increase plant utilization to in-
      crease gross margins and decrease excess plant
      capacity.

The first two strategic roles were most important to the overall
mission of the new product program. Products A and B did
meet the two roles. There may be some question as to whether
the first two products were financially successful relative to the
original forecast, but there is no question that they were highly
successful in defending market position and preempting foreign competition from gaining headway in the category. Thus,
for two of the three new products developed, performance appears strong from both a financial and a strategic standpoint.
The real problem was that too few new products got out the
door. Maybe management only wanted winners, so only the top
three new products were launched. Or maybe resources were so
scarce that three new products were all that could be handled
internally. Whatever the reason, the message is that what was
done in new products was good, just not enough, at least relative to the objectives set for the new product program. Of
course, the final variable missing from this stage of analysis is
the payback. If the company invested $25 million to accomplish
this program, our whole view of the relative success of those
three new products would change dramatically.

    Thus defining success and failure of new products is highly
interpretive. The good news is that keeping track of how well
each new product is doing as well as the portfolio of products
is the best way to establish a database, which will then provide
a tool to use in forecasting for the future. The bad news is that
top management will often use those original forecasts as a
club, not a tool.

Determine the Underlying Causes Behind Each New Product's Success or Failure

Accurate information is often difficult to collect in this step because underlying reasons behind performance change radi-

EXHIBIT 3.6 Financial Performance of Product A

Total Products	Forecast	Actual	Variance
Cumulative revenues	$ 22,000,000	$ 6,546,000	- 70 %
Cumulative profits	2,500,000	512,100	- 80
PRODUCT A			
Year 1 revenues	400,000	550,000	+ 38
Year 1 profits	32,000	(64,000)	-300
Year 2 revenues	460,000	635,000	+ 38
Year 2 profits	41,400	50,800	+ 23
Year 3 revenues	525,000	700,000	+ 33
Year 3 profits	52,500	56,000	+ 7
Cumulative revenues	$ 1,385,000	$1,885,000	+ 36 %
Cumulative profits	$ 125,900	$ 42,800	- 66 %

EXHIBIT 3.7 Financial Performance of Product B

Total Products	Forecast	Actual	Variance
PRODUCT B			
Year 1 revenues	$ 1,500,000	$ 950,000	- 37 %
Year 1 profits	120,000	95,000	- 21
Year 2 revenues	1,800,000	1,140,000	- 37
Year 2 profits	160,000	165,000	+ 3
Year 3 revenues	2,160,000	1,425,000	- 34
Year 3 profits	216,000	211,000	- 2
Cumulative revenues	$ 5,460,000	$ 3,515,000	- 36 %
Cumulative profits	$ 496,000	$ 471,000	- 5 %

EXHIBIT 3.8 Financial Performance of Product C

Total Products	Forecast	Actual	Variance
PRODUCT C			
Year 1 revenues	$ 500,000	$ 250,000	- 50 %
Year 1 profits	40,000	(55,000)	- 238
Year 2 revenues	600,000	480,000	- 20
Year 2 profits	600,000	33,500	- 44
Year 3 revenues	700,000	416,000	- 41
Year 3 profits	70,000	20,800	- 70
Cumulative revenues	$1,800,000	$ 1,146,000	- 36 %
Cumulative profits	$ 710,000	$ (700)	N/A

---

cally, depending upon whether the product was a success or a failure. Information becomes interpretative, and reasons often are interdependent. The reasons why new products succeed or fail can usually be attributed to insufficient market research or to internal problems in execution, planning, testing, positioning, or forecasting. For example, competitive responses to a new product launch can negatively affect projections, but usually a product failure could have turned into a success with better internal planning and execution.

The areas that should be examined to understand why a new product performed as it did include:

✧ Assumptions made in business analysis and interpretation of test results. How did information differ from observations that can now be made in the market?

✧ Data and analysis behind original financial forecasts; reasons behind changes made to forecast after test market. What is the variance between original forecasts, projections after test market,

and actual performance? External and internal
factors also affect the performance.

✧ External factors that influenced performance:
consumer demand shifts, competitive responses,
distribution channel requirements.

✧ Internal factors that influenced performance:
lack of proper funding, insufficient research, inadequate testing, no screening criteria; positive,
strong sponsorship, technology and marketing
cooperation, or top management commitment.

✧ Quality of execution and coordination of the
product launch in the marketplace.

Frequently, looking at the business analysis and test market results can show the reason for a new product's performance. If
the new product is an underachiever, the cause may be competitive moves, such as raising the stakes by cutting price,
adding promotions, or increasing advertising spending. Or perhaps the new product concept did not have a well-defined
need premise or a clearly defined positioning that the consumer could easily relate to and understand.

Assumptions behind original objectives set for a new product often do not relate to test market results—another reason
for new product failures. Then why run a test market? The
major purpose of a test market is to simulate performance in
the marketplace before costly rollout expenditures. However,
over-optimism frequently creeps into financial objective setting. When a new product does well in a test, management
often assumes that with some incremental spending, volume
can double. Replicating performance in a test market is one
thing. Doubling it is usually a prescription for disappointment.
Other times, the numbers increase to justify the manufacturing
capital investment that has already been made. And the many
different reasons continue.

Every good analysis of new products must include competitive contingency plans that spell out how competition may respond to the launch of a company's new product. Managers
often fail to anticipate what corrective measures will need to
be taken to counteract competitors' moves against a new prod-

uct. Will competition increase advertising dollars, encourage dealer discounts, drop the price, and launch a competitive "better-than" new product? This shortsightedness about the effect of competition is a key reason why new products fail to perform to the original forecasts. Other times a new product is launched before its time, when too small a segment of consumers is interested in the product. For example, microwave popcorn and the microwave itself were products that had to wait for the world to recognize their value.

Internal factors are often the cause of a new product's success or failure. The sales force didn't sell the new product aggressively enough, and therefore when the advertising ran, the product still was not on the shelf. Or there were manufacturing problems with the product as volume increased, because as through-put went up, the existing equipment could not supply adequate demand for the product. In contrast, the success of a product may be due to the technological breakthrough that came from the R&D lab or to astute marketing that positioned the product dramatically differently from competition.

The actual launch of a product can be the factor that spells success or failure. Was the product promoted correctly? Was there enough consumer awareness building behind it to stimulate trial? Were distributors and dealers given adequate incentives? Had enough consumer testing been done prior to launch to work out the bugs in the product before it got into the hands of the consumer?

An industrial equipment manufacturer launched a new product that was priced at $15,000 and had been tested with only two users. Both users were satisfied with the product, so the company decided to launch it nationally. However, the type of oil used by other customers caused the product to shut down automatically: The product ended up as a major failure.

Another company selling a diskette product had estimated the market growth at five times the actual, had not thoroughly tested the product, and had not anticipated that competitors would drop their price. Nor was the sales force committed to selling the product. Why should they? The new diskette product offered less than half the commission rate that the regular product line provided to them. Again, the product failed.

One may question how a new product can be launched in

spite of these obvious barriers. That's the downside of having strong product champions who have an emotional attachment to new products. The irony is that although a company cannot live without product champions, there must also be enough checks and balances in the process so that sound business judgment—not emotion—drive new product decisions.

In short, determining the reasons behind each new product's performance shows what internal strengths were exploited and which weaknesses need to be overcome or compensated for. Moreover, the real benefit in examining the causes behind performance comes in identifying consistent patterns that may emerge across new products.

The most common reasons behind a failing new product include:

- ✧ Lack of clear up-front financial and strategic objectives that define what the new product is expected to accomplish resulting in overoptimistic financial forecasts.
- ✧ Inadequate market research, product-performance testing, and market testing; insufficient business analysis and inadequate understanding of competition.
- ✧ Lack of marketing programs that appropriately support the product's launch.
- ✧ Lack of product differentiation.
- ✧ Insufficient involvement of other departments during the development and launch of the product.

Thus, by identifying similar patterns behind new product performance, management is better equipped to know what changes need to be made to improve the effectiveness of the company's new product program.

Evaluate the Payback Period

Evaluating the payback period simply means identifying the breakeven point: When did the new product's operating profits exceed the costs required for developing it? This step is diffi-

EXHIBIT 3.9 New Product Financials for a Specialty Chemicals Manufacturer

	Year 1	Year 2	Year 3	Year 4	Year 5
Cumulative revenues	$2,500,000	$4,700,000	$9,500,000	$17,600,000	$28,400,000
Cumulative profits	150,000	375,000	875,000	1,950,000	3,650,000
Capital investments	(250,000)	(600,000)	(1,000,000)	(1,150,000)	(1,200,000)
Development costs	(250,000)	(600,000)	(850,000)	(1,000,000)	(1,250,000)
Total costs	$ (500,000)	$(1,200,000)	$(1,850,000)	$(2,150,000)	$(2,450,000)
Variance (profit minus total cost)	$ (350,000)	$ (825,000)	$ (975,000)	$ (200,000)	$ 1,200,000

cult, because the growth path of a new product is always tough to determine. The reason managers are often reluctant to measure payback is that it is difficult to determine the length of a new product's life cycle.

Too often management is either too impatient to see a return on a new product or too lackadaisical to measure payback. The impatient ones need to develop a greater understanding of a new product's growth-and-profit cycle. One way to accomplish this "learning" is to demonstrate the growth cycle taken by new products during a five- or ten-year period. In turn, management may become a bit more sensitized to the longer-term nature of new products.

The next step is to do a "roll-up" of the payback for the total new product portfolio. (See Exhibit 3.9.)

Keep in mind that payback periods are often set by new product type in order to differentiate the relative risk, growth path, and level of investment required for each. A line extension or new addition may require, for one company, a two-year payback period, in contrast to a new-to-the-world product that has a five-year payback period and a new-to-the-company product with a four-year payback period by the same company. Therefore, it is important when calculating payback periods to group the results by new product type.

The final exercise is determining the amount of time required

EXHIBIT 3.10 Example of Development Time for Three New Products

	Product A (Months)	Product B (Months)	Product C (Months)
Concept development	3	5	2
Business analysis	3	4	4
Prototype development	8	4	16
Test market	6	2	8
Launch	3	5	4
Total development time	23	20	34

to get each new product from concept generation to commercialization. Take, for example, a transportation company that has broken out the time required to launch three new products.

On average, it appears to take this company approximately two years to move new products from concept development to market commercialization. However, this development period is relevant only when compared to competition and the industry. Some industries may typically require seven to eight years to develop a new product, because of technology and capital investments. If your company can develop a new product that is new to the company in three years, and your key competitor successfully accomplishes the same thing in eighteen months, your development process may be taking too long.

Development time is an important factor to consider when forecasting future new product revenues. With a five-year forecast, the new product revenue stream will not even begin until year 3 if it takes two years before any new product gets launched. Granted, there may be several new products that are worked on simultaneously during the first couple of years and will be launched in years 3 and 4, but the point is still an important one. It takes time to develop new products, and during that time cash is only flowing *out*, not in. Moreover, other investment opportunities may be foregone in lieu of the products under development.

EXHIBIT 3.11 Allocation of Management Time Spent on Development of New Products

	Number of People	Number of Days per Month per Person	Percentage of Time Spent on New Products per Person
Senior management	6	0.5	3%
New product management	2	20	100
Marketing management	3	4	20
Research & development	5	8	40
Manufacturing	2	4	20
Engineering	2	3	15
Finance	1	2	10
Total	21	41.5	

There is one other time issue that should be examined. How much time did all participants in the process spend on new products? That requires an estimate of what portion of each employee's time by functional area is spent on new products during an average month. (See Exhibit 3.11.)

If later in the diagnostic audit it appears that manufacturing the new product is a frequent problem area, the reason may be that manufacturing and engineering are not involved enough in the process. Moreover, if the new product objectives keep changing every quarter, it may be an indication that some senior managers need to spend more than a half day a month just getting up to speed on the new product projects. The time commitment of a few may be too short, while the involvement of others may actually be too long. The point is to identify the specific resource requirements needed to get the job done and then ensure that sufficient time is allocated to the effort by functional area.

Knowing who spends time on new products often reveals the functional strengths that are exploited in successful new products. Very often there is a direct relationship between the causes of success or failure of a new product and the amount of functional time committed to that product. If R&D spends the most time on them, new products are more often technology driven. If marketing is the major participant in the process, new products may be more advertising driven. There needs to be an appropriate balance between functions so that internal strengths are utilized to cover as many bases as possible.

Identify the Internal Strengths of the Top Three Competitors

The first step is to identify your top two or three competitors. Then develop the list of competitors for each new product launched, and list the type and number of new products each competitor developed during the same time period. This information can be relatively easily obtained through annual reports and 10-Ks, trade associations, periodicals, and phone calls to security analysts, suppliers, and vendors. It's easy to brag about the three great new line extensions that have been launched by your company until you begin to assess what your competition has done.

Now compare the external survival rates of a competitor's products to your own company's new product survival rate. While you won't get a true evaluation of that competitor's internal new product success rate, you will get a reasonable proxy. Also, be sure to evaluate the reasons behind varying success rates.

The major advantage of identifying competitors' new product activity is to get an idea of how they might respond to new products that are launched in their category arenas. It is important to compare the number, type, and survival rate of competitors' new products. It is beneficial to compare these measurements to internal past performance as well as to companies in other industries that perform well overall in new products.

New Product Performance Recap

So far we have collected information aimed at providing a quantitative assessment of how well a company's new products have performed. Let's summarize some of the performance

EXHIBIT 3.12 Recap of New Products Performance

Number of new products launched during a five-year period	10 new products
Number of new products planned for launch	12
Revenues and profits by type of new products commercialized (percent of revenues shown)	
New to the world	30%
New to the company	40%
Line extensions	20%
Repositioned products	10%
Cumulative revenues generated from new products	$5,000,000
Cumulative profits generated from new products	$600,000
External survival rate	80%
Internal success rate relative to original goals	50%
Actual new product revenues as a percent of forecast revenues	92%
Actual new product profits as a percent of forecast profits	57%
New product revenues as a percent of corporate revenues	10%
New product revenues as a percent of corporate revenue growth	65%
Corporate growth rate during the past five years	12%
Corporate growth rate without new products	1%
New product profits as a percent of corporate profits	12%
Total development costs and capital investments	$350,000
Payback period	year 4
Average development time for each new product	24 months
Number of new products launched by competitor 1	5
Survival rate of competitor 1	80%
Number of new products launched by competitor 2	3
Survival rate of competitor 2	67%

measures that have been discussed. The value of interpreting the performance data in total is that additional observations can be made and a better understanding established regarding why and how new products have performed in the past. By now the following new product statistics can be assembled. Take, for example, an industrial tractor company that has $50 million in sales and has launched ten new products in the past five years. After analyzing past performance, the diagnosis was that overall new product performance was excellent. Here is a summary of the performance benchmarks for this industrial company as depicted in Exhibit 3.12.

Each indicator offers critical information on how well the new product program is working. If the internal success rate is 50 percent, the causes behind performance need further examination. The causes may range from unrealistic forecasts to low spending for marketing support. The historical new product performance statistics should be used as a tool to help pinpoint past strengths on which to capitalize and weaknesses to overcome.

Conducting an annual historical new product performance analysis provides a mechanism for monitoring progress from one year to the next. This is often a valuable tool for securing additional resources and dollars for future new products. In the next example (Exhibit 3.13), we examine a $325 million consumer products division within a $3 billion corporation. The example shows why an audit is important. Big revenues stemming from new products can easily fool management. During a five-year period, the consumer products division launched thirty-five new products, which generated $66 million in cumulative revenues, representing 20 percent of total division revenues. Thus, division management was touting the significant revenue role that new products played in its growth, but total cumulative profits from those thirty-five new products amounted to $89,000: $66 million in sales generated only $89,000 in *pretax profits*.

Since approximately $6.5 million had been invested in the new product program, it is clear that this division did not have a successful new product program from a profit standpoint. After further examination, one of the causes behind its poor profit performance is the predominant number of very small revenue generators. Nearly 60 percent of the new products had less than $1 million in cumulative sales, and 72 percent generated less than $500,000 in cumulative profits during the five-year period. When the profit losers were added to the new products that enjoyed some profits, albeit small, the total was $89,000. Furthermore, over 40 percent of all new products launched were either profit losers or broke even at best. Only

EXHIBIT 3.13 CUMULATIVE REVENUES AND PROFITS ANALYSIS

Cumulative Five-Year Revenues	Number of New Products	Percent of Total Launched
$0 to $500,000	14	40%
$500,000 to $1,000,000	6	17
$1,000,000 to $2,000,000	5	14
Over $2,000,000	10	29
Total	35	100%

Cumulative Five-Year Profits		
Losers	5	14%
Breakevens	10	29
$0 to $500,000	15	43
$500,000 to $1,000,000	2	6
Over $1,000,000	3	8
Total	35	100%

five out of thirty-five new products generated more than $500,000 in cumulative five-year profits.

An analysis of performance by product type helps to identify the reasons underlying overall performance. (See Exhibit 3.14.) By analyzing performance by product type, one of the major causes of poor performance becomes apparent: with new-to-the-world and line extensions, the company had a technological edge that provided functional benefits to consumers, Thus sales volume was strong in these two categories. However, the company never really paid any attention to unit costs, and as a result, these new product types were running at a margin far below existing products. Moreover, with the new-to-the-company products, they put together some rather poorly executed marketing and advertising programs that did not differentiate their products from competition.

EXHIBIT 3.14 Cumulative Sales and Profits by New Product Type

	Sales	Profits	Losses
New-to-the-world	$ 25,982,000	$ 243,000	
New-to-the-company	11,493,000	0	$ (919,000)
Line extensions	25,551,000	765,000	
Repositioning	3,220,000	0	
Total	$ 66,246,000	$ 1,008,000	$ (919,000)
Net Profit		$ 89,000	

Assessment of Strengths and Weaknesses

Identifying those internal strengths and weaknesses relevant to building new products is highly subjective, qualitative, and difficult. It is an evaluation open to a high degree of interpretation and judgment. The farther away a company moves from its existing strengths, the greater the degree of risk becomes. That is not to say that the company should not take risks by going outside their identified pool of strengths, but even new-to-the-world products can draw on internal strengths. This might be in the form of a technology application or brand name equity that will bring perceived value to the product; a proprietary manufacturing process that can be utilized in making the new product; or management expertise or familiarity with a given category that can be applied in developing new products.

The assessment of any internal strength must be made relative to its contribution to the company's competitive advantage, which means that a sound understanding of competitors' advantages and vulnerabilities is mandatory. Some major areas to consider are the new product strategic context, the new product development process, the measurement and tracking system, communication across functional areas, and organizational issues such as people, culture, risk, structure, rewards, and commitment.

The best way to conduct this assessment is on a category-by-category basis. After a food company had selected four categories in which to pursue new product development, it found that one in particular offered immense opportunities to utilize existing strengths. Two other categories afforded some internal leverage, and the fourth seemed really far afield from any internal advantages. So the priorities were set for competitive advantage concerns.

Of course, strengths vary from company to company, but they tend to fall into four common groups: cost and manufacturing; technology; demand; and marketing, sales, and distribution. For each of the groups, there is an expanded list of attributes. (See Exhibit 3.15.)

The next step in the audit is to decide, on a scale of 1 to 10, how well your company's attributes stack up in any given market category compared to your key competitor. First, identify a set of key competitive attributes. Then apply the following scale to each attribute. A score of 1 signifies a significant competitive disadvantage over you in that market category; 2 signifies relative equality; and 3 indicates a very strong competitive advantage.

This scoring approach is suggested only as a means to compare degrees of strength by category. While this analysis can clearly be done qualitatively, applying quantitative rankings to the factors requires more thought, allows for simpler comparison, and gives concrete form to sometimes abstract ideas. While this system is a bit relative, any significant and thorough list of attributes with a total score of less than 30 percent of the total possible score (e.g., 27 on a scale of 90) means trouble. A score of more than 60 percent of the total possible (e.g., 54 on a scale of 90) suggest a solid base of strength.

After completing this assessment, you will have a picture of how your company stacks up against competition in terms of new product building blocks. Now you are ready to examine how well your company looks in terms of the key success factors for effective new product development. These factors are those most commonly found in companies that have a proven track record of hitting their new product targets.

EXHIBIT 3.15 Strengths-and-Weaknesses Assessment for a Market Category Compared to Top Competitor

Company Strengths
Compared to
Top Competitor
(Score 1–3)

Cost-Related and Manufacturing Factors

1. Low-cost producer: Role that unit cost plays in the profitability of the product line. Low-cost producer scores 3; high-cost producer scores 1. _____

2. Patented processes: Degree to which patented processes provide a genuine competitive advantage that cannot be easily duplicated or is costly to replicate. _____

3. Automated equipment: Importance of robotics and automated machinery in achieving cost economies. Compare burden or overhead costs of competitor's cost structure. _____

4. Low material cost: Portion of raw materials in cost stream; determine competitor with low-cost materials advantage. _____

5. Low-cost labor: Portion of labor costs in cost stream; identify competitor with low labor costs. _____

6. Unique source of supply: Determine relative substitution capabilities of raw materials and competitive strongholds with suppliers. _____

7. Productivity programs: Compare competitor's formalized activities and programs in cost reduction and productivity enhancements. _____

TECHNOLOGY-DRIVEN FACTORS

8. Product patents: Patented products score 3. Products without patents score 1 if patented product exists, if not, then score 2. _____

9. Design patents: Score 3 if design patents exist and are a key advantage in the manufacturing process; score 2 if they exist but are not important; score 1 if they do not exist. _____

10. CAD/CAM systems: Assess competitor's use of CAD/CAM and degree of importance of design adaptability and efficiency. _____

11. R&D spending: Competitor spending most in R&D scores 3, the least scores 1; weighting determined by effect R&D has had on new products developed in past within category. _____

DEMAND-RELATED AND MARKETING FACTORS

12. Product differentiation: The degree of perceived uniqueness of proposed product line that can be developed relative to existing offerings. _____

13. Price advantage: Lowest price in market scores 3; highest price scores 1. _____

14. Packaging advantage: The contribution of packaging in stimulating purchase—unique design or protective qualities. _____

15. Advertising expenditures and exposures: Importance of advertising in motivating purchase intent and total advertising dollars spent, and reach and frequency achieved by competitor. _____

16. Advertising creative: Level of aided and unaided recall by consumer and degree to which any one competitor's creative has built awareness of the category. _____

17. Distribution network: Role that channel management and multi-channel distribution play in product-offering success. _____

18. Promotion impact: The importance of consumer promotions and trade discounts in moving product off the shelf; compare competitor's spending levels for each. _____

19. Public relations: To what extent does publicity influence consumer trial-and-repeat purchase of the product? _____

20. Focused market niche: How does each competitor position its product within the category? Who has the most memorable and useful positioning? _____

21. Brand-name recognition: Degree to which brand name is major factor influencing purchase; competitor with highest brand-name awareness and perceived price/value benefit scores 3. _____

22. Loyal consumer base: A competitor who has strong consumer franchise scores 3. _____

23. Management expertise: Tangible and recognizable experience by managers in category that will provide a competitive advantage. _____

24. Market research: Already completed market research that will offer insights into a category—especially good if research is too costly for competition to conduct. _____

SALES AND DISTRIBUTION FACTORS

25. Sales-coverage breadth: Geographic penetration and sales force coverage—importance of broad sales coverage in selling product. _____

26. Channel and distribution-cost advantage: Low-cost distributor scores 3; high-cost distributor scores 1. _____

27. Selling costs: Cost per sales call and selling costs per revenue dollar generated relative to competitor. _____

28. Market/buyer clout: Degree to which other product-line offerings or trade relationships give a competitor an edge in the category with buyers. _____

29. Delivery turnaround time: Extent to which quick delivery is important to buyers in the category. _____

30. Strategic distribution centers: Geographic coverage of distribution centers that are strategically positioned to offer lower shipping costs and better delivery times. _____

TOTAL _____

Best Practice Scoreboard

Among companies that are successful at developing new products there emerges a set of common attributes that influence success. This is not to suggest that successful companies always embody these attributes, nor does it suggest that the only way to become successful is to adopt all these characteristics. However, for the most part, companies that do have certain attributes in place are most apt to succeed in their new product efforts. You can judge how well your own company stacks up by answering the questions in Exhibit 3.16. Score each factor as follows:

❖ Score 2 points if attribute is currently in place and working effectively.

❖ Score 1 point if attribute has just recently been established.

❖ Score 0 if attribute does not exist in the organization.

Based on the fifteen best-practice characteristics, the highest score attainable in this stage is 30 points. Companies that fall above 20 to 25 tend to have the internal tools in place to succeed at new products. Companies scoring in the 15-to-20 range have some strong points working for them but need to examine ways to improve their internal new product operations. Companies that score less than 15 need to carefully examine ways to improve their process and overall approach to new products.

Again, do not take these success factors as the pills for immediate cure of a previously failing new product program. Even after companies have changed their programs to include them, it may take one to two years to see some definite progress made in the new product effort.

There is no easy way out. To perform well in new products there are few substitutes for having these factors in place. It requires planning, thinking through where you want the new product program to head, committed resources, thorough homework, consistency in approach, and rewards for the doers based upon how well new products perform in the marketplace.

The final part of the diagnostic audit is assessing the relative degree of top management commitment behind the new product development program. This one is the most difficult to evaluate. Often what top managers say is not quite reality. If top management is just not dedicated to new products, try to change that. But if after your attempt, no change results, stop banging your head against a wall and transfer to a new division, department, or company. The chances of succeeding when management is not standing firmly behind new products are limited.

Top Management Commitment

Once again, I invite you to judge your company, this time on top management commitment. (See Exhibit 3.17.) The question being asked is whether top management is "behind" new products in terms of a willingness to invest, accept risk, and allocate the needed funds and talent required to make it work. And as important as the "tone" that top management sets, the attitude toward new products that is communicated throughout the or-

EXHIBIT 3.16 Best-Practice Scoreboard

	Success Attributes
1. Strategic-planning process: Does the company use a formalized strategy for strategic planning?	_____
2. Growth role for new products: Does the corporate-growth plan include a definition of the role of internally developed new products during the next five years?	_____
3. Defined new product strategy: Is there a well-defined new product strategy in writing that identifies the financial gap, strategic roles, and screening criteria that new products must satisfy?	_____
4. Screening criteria: Are financial and strategic performance screens established to evaluate new product concepts? Are screens based on associated risk by new product type?	_____
5. Step-by-step new product process and consistent execution: Has the company had a systematic and formalized, yet flexible and adaptive, new product process in place for at least five years?	_____
6. Idea generation after homework has been completed: Does idea generation begin after external market niches have been identified, needs and wants explored, attractive categories to compete in determined, and internal competitive strengths assessed?	_____
7. Monitoring and tracking systems: Does the company formally monitor and track new products relative to original objectives and measure cost per introduction?	_____
8. Incentive programs: Are there compensation programs that encourage an entrepreneurial attitude, reward risk takers, and reinforce innovative thinking?	_____
9. Clear lines of responsibility: Is there a clear understanding of who is responsible for new products and who is held accountable for performance? Is the decision-making process understood and are approval points clearly identified and adhered to?	_____
10. Top management commitment: Does top management provide consistent commitment to new products in funding and allocate the best managers, with high-powered skills and know-how, to the new product effort?	_____
11. Separate new product organization: Does the primary new product activity take place in an independent group that is set apart from existing business management?	_____

12. Entrepreneurial spirit: Is there a willingness to take risks and an eagerness to break new ground and engender an independent spirit?   _____

13. Product fit with internal strengths: Do the majority of new products play off or draw upon existing strengths?   _____

14. Product advocates or champions: Are there people in the company, either self-selected or assigned, who are the sparks for shepherding the development of new products?   _____

15. Adaptive new product organization: Does the company change the new product organization to accommodate the role and objectives set for new products by matching new product type by structure required?   _____

TOTAL   _____

---

ganization is the key. As emphasized in Chapter 1, top management commitment is one of the ten vital success factors.

For each of the fifteen factors score either 2 points or 0. Thirty points is the highest possible score, and committed managers usually fall into the 20 points-or-more range. If the score is lower than 20, then the specific indicators need to be further examined to determine the "real" degree of commitment. A score below 10 suggests that it may be time to hang it up.

In Summary

A diagnostic audit is an invaluable tool for correcting discovered weaknesses, better utilizing strengths, and making your new product program work. It also provides the framework for realistic expectations for future new products. In particular, it sets the stage for development of your new product blueprint and new product strategy—in other words, the very cornerstone of your program. The diagnostic audit can usually be completed in about three months, depending upon availability of data, access to management, and number and quality of resources assigned to the audit. The point is that the time required to conduct the audit is relatively short and yet can provide insights and recommended changes that will affect a company's new product program for years to come.

How a company uses the results of a new product diagnostic

EXHIBIT 3.17 Top Management Commitment

Management
Commitment

1. Long-term profitability: Emphasized more than short-term quarterly performance. _____

2. Risk-taking environment fostered: A willingness to play a long-shot from time to time and an acceptance of at least a 30-to-40 percent failure rate from commercialized new products. _____

3. Effective communication: This is essential if the company is to establish objectives, measure accomplishment, raise morale, and encourage commitment. _____

4. Willingness to accept failure: An attitude that acknowledges the inherent risk of developing and launching new products. _____

5. Consistent and visible commitment of funds and resources for new products: The important word here is consistent. It is not sufficient to commit human resources or financial support on a sporadic basis. _____

6. Adherence to formal planning process: This requires more than establishing a process on paper; it must not be given just lip service but must be the major instrument of guidance and control in the company. _____

7. Reliance on strategic and financial-screening criteria: They provide a common set of determinants for choosing between one new product idea and another. They also provide an objective measure of acceptability or success, which otherwise may become quixotic and unreliable. _____

8. Flexibility in the new product process: Despite the need for a formally defined process, management must be willing to change direction and move quickly to take advantage of competitive moves, discoveries, or market changes. It may sometimes be necessary to skip steps in the formalized process. _____

9. Dependence upon technology to drive new products: In general, technology tends to produce more and better competitively advantaged products than superficial or cosmetic changes. _____

10. Linking of marketing, manufacturing, and distribution: All aspects of the development effort are important to successful new products. One cannot neglect any part of the chain without endangering success. _____

11. Encouragement of an entrepreneurial attitude: Individuals are given freedom and authority to make decisions on their own and are truly held accountable for new product performance.   _____

12. Longevity of new product managers and participants: Keep key new product people in place for at least three to five years. Make the new product function a career path.   _____

13. Rewards for risk takers and performers: The people who take the risks get the recognition—psychological and financial—in title and salary that their performance deserves.   _____

14. Reinforcement for innovative managers: The middle managers responsible for new product development are encouraged to break new ground in their management styles and approaches.   _____

15. Autonomy for new product managers: Managers have authority as well as responsibility, without constant overseeing and second-guessing by top management.   _____

TOTAL   _____

---

audit is highly dependent upon the reasons the audit was conducted in the first place. An attitude of trust, openness, and interest in understanding past performance must underscore top management's desire for an audit. It cannot be used as a club to control the new product budget. It should, on the other hand, be used as a vehicle to explore how best to improve the effectiveness of dollars spent and people assigned to the new product development process. It provides a valuable information base for getting a new product program turned around. Managers may begin to get involved in the audit and generate some excitement for creating a new process or organization. Consequently, a certain degree of momentum is created, ownership encouraged, and commitment somewhat established. The mere conduct of a diagnostic audit is a signal to managers that top management may at least be willing to look at ways to improve the approaches taken to new products. Sometimes the key benefit is not the information derived from an audit but rather the enthusiasm and interest that is rekindled into the new product culture.

Interpretation of the results is difficult. It requires association making similar to that needed in effective concept generation. Thus launching plans for a successful new product program start as soon as the audit begins.

With the information from the new product diagnostic audit the company can now begin to formulate a new product strategy. When developing the strategy management can use the audit to reduce the relative risk inherent in new products. The strategy must capitalize on the company's strengths and circumvent weak areas, while the shortfalls are addressed and remedied.

Appendix
Diagnostic Audit Example

A real-world example of a diagnostic audit for a $400 million medical device company follows. It represents three months of effort.

For this $400 million company, the new product diagnostic audit produced several key findings:

✧ The company has enjoyed roughly a four-fold return on their dollar investments in new products.

✧ Recently, though, the company has exhibited a decline in newness in the type of new products launched.

✧ There are a few key areas that will improve the company's new product efficiency and effectiveness.

From 1994 to 1999, this company spent approximately $74 million on R&D investments. (See Exhibit 3.18.) From those investments, this company received roughly a four-fold return based on cumulative R&D dollars to gross profits generated from new products. (See Exhibits 3.19 a and b). Much of this company's growth in sales and profits can be attributed to new products. Cumulatively, from 1994 to 1999, new products represented 52 percent of sales and 47 percent of profits. (See Exhibit 3.20.) Through the years, new products launched since

1994 have grown from 5 percent to 75 percent of total revenue. (See Exhibits 3.21 a and b.) Over the past 10 years this company has achieved a relatively balanced portfolio of new product types as shown in Exhibit 3.22. However, breaking down that ten-year period into two parts reveals a different picture. (See Exhibit 3.23.) From 1989 to 1994, over 40 percent of the new products launched carried a high degree of newness (new to the world and new to the company). From 1995 to 1999, less than 15 percent were new to the world and new to the company, thus indicating a decline in newness.

This company's situation is beginning to become clear. They have enjoyed successful financial performance based on the dollars they have invested in new products and how well those products have done in the market. Recently, however, a majority of products launched have been line extensions and improvements. Typically, these products carry lower risk but also lower return. In this company's case, they have been able to launch very profitable line extensions and improvements, but that has disguised the company's move away from totally new products. This trend may not have caused any alarm except that the company has been losing market share to competitors because of the competitor's ability to launch more new-to-the-world products.

Often one new product will spawn additional new-product offspring. This offers an excellent incentive for the company to redirect some of its R&D efforts back to new-to-the-world and new-to-the-company products. Exhibit 3.24 indicates that one of the company's original new-to-the-world products spawned next-generation line extensions and improvements that have added greatly to the value of the overall product line. Without the new-to-the-world product, the company would not have been able to contribute the additional $32 million in net sales. It is important to note, however, that incrementally each additional next generation's net cumulative sales contribution has been less. This builds a strong case for the company to begin focusing again on a higher degree of newness in their products.

Exhibits 3.25 and 3.26 a and b provide further support for increasing newness, because the company will not be able to sustain its financial performance just with line extensions and improvements. As seen in Exhibit 3.25, first-year sales of new products have varied from year to year but have declined over-all. The jump in 1996 was due to the launch of a major new product. Exhibits 3.26 a and b indicate that line extensions and improvements are still marginally profitable, yet they con-tribute heavily to overall company profits because of the high volume of products sold.

Therefore, the overall picture for this company is that of a successful new product player who focused heavily on new-to-the-world and new-to-the-company products in its early years. They have been able to enjoy an exhilarating new prod-uct ride for nearly ten years. Recently, however, the competi-tive environment has intensified, and there is a need to redirect efforts towards some newer products. Already there have been a few indications that the existing line extensions and improvements are losing some of their power.

The qualitative research for this diagnostic audit also un-covered some ideas for improving new product efficiency and effectiveness. This company has been in a high-growth cycle for its ten-year existence. It has been able to perform success-fully in new products. But ad hoc planning, an undisciplined product development process, and a rather random approach to new products will require some tightening. This company

EXHIBIT 3.18 R&D Spending

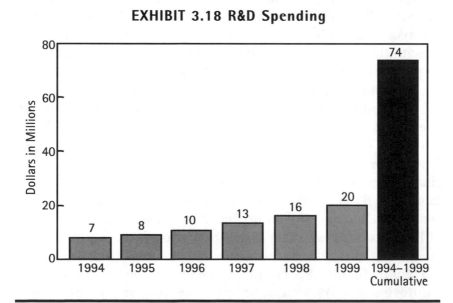

EXHIBIT 3.19a Sales from New Products Launched Since 1994

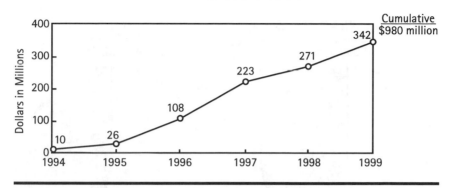

EXHIBIT 3.19b Gross Profits from New Products Launched Since 1994

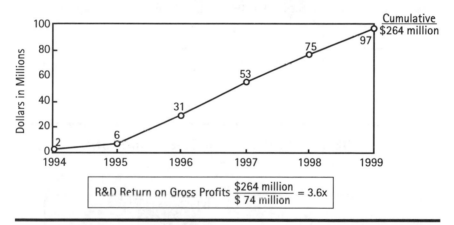

has reached a level in its own growth cycle where it must establish and adhere to one, commonly agreed-upon and understood, formalized development process. Most important, at each stage of the process there should be clearly stated accountabilities and necessary data collection and analysis, as well as approval points for deciding whether to proceed to the next stage with each project.

Establishing a tracking and measurement system can be a critical link for ensuring effective implementation of a formalized process. It is important to stress that the system should

EXHIBIT 3.20 New Products Contribution

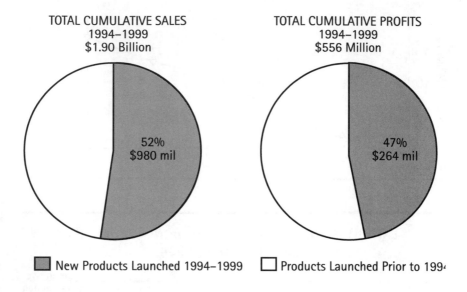

TOTAL CUMULATIVE SALES
1994–1999
$1.90 Billion

52%
$980 mil

TOTAL CUMULATIVE PROFITS
1994–1999
$556 Million

47%
$264 mil

■ New Products Launched 1994–1999   □ Products Launched Prior to 1994

EXHIBIT 3.21a Growth in Sales and Profits

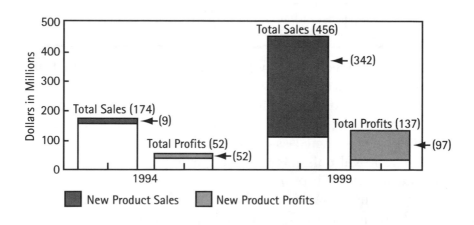

Dollars in Millions

Total Sales (456)

◄(342)

Total Sales (174)
◄(9)

Total Profits (52)
◄(52)

Total Profits (137)
◄(97)

1994   1999

■ New Product Sales   ■ New Product Profits

EXHIBIT 3.21b Company X Total Sales

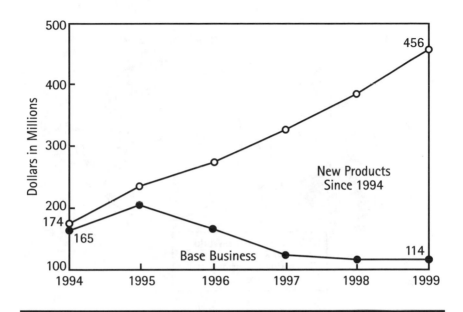

EXHIBIT 3.22 New Products Launched

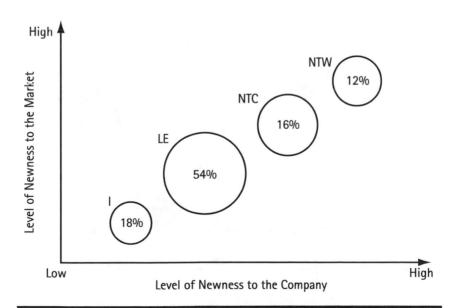

EXHIBIT 3.23 Newness Factor

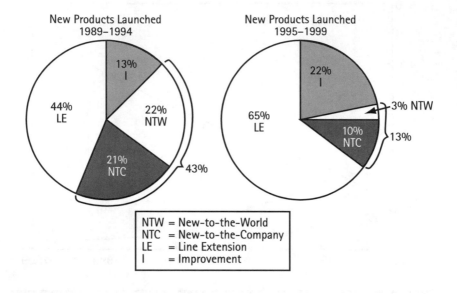

New Products Launched
1989–1994

13%
I

44%
LE

22%
NTW

21%
NTC

43%

New Products Launched
1995–1999

22%
I

65%
LE

3% NTW

10%
NTC

13%

NTW = New-to-the-World
NTC = New-to-the-Company
LE = Line Extension
I   = Improvement

EXHIBIT 3.24 Next Generation Example

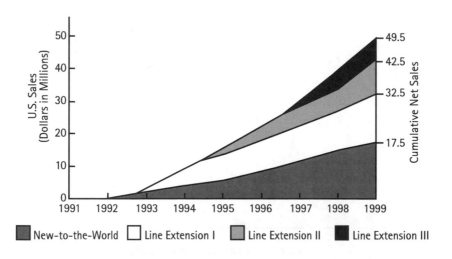

50

40

30

20

10

0

U.S. Sales
(Dollars in Millions)

49.5

42.5

32.5

17.5

Cumulative Net Sales

1991 1992 1993 1994 1995 1996 1997 1998 1999

■ New-to-the-World   □ Line Extension I   ■ Line Extension II   ■ Line Extension III

EXHIBIT 3.25 First-Year Sales

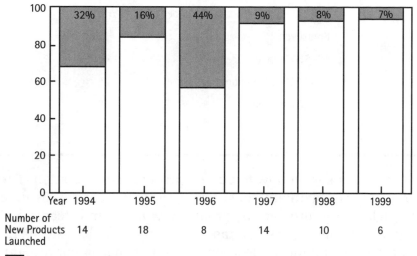

Year	1994	1995	1996	1997	1998	1999
Number of New Products Launched	14	18	8	14	10	6

Sales from New Products

EXHIBIT 3.26a 1994–99 Cumulative Sales of New Products

	Number	% of Total
$0–$500,000	28	40%
$500,000–$1 million	12	17
$1–$2 million	10	14
$2–$3 million	8	11
Over $3 million	12	17

measure both project and overall company effectiveness and efficiency in new products. A measurement and tracking system should be used as a *tool* for assuring future success of a company's new product efforts, not as a club to measure productivity levels. (See Exhibit 3.27.)

There are a few organization improvements that will also enhance the new process and the new product program in general. Training new product participants is necessary in order to

EXHIBIT 3.26b 1994–99 Cumulative Profits of New Products

	Number	% of Total
Breakeven	20	29%
$0–$500,000	30	43
$500,000–$1 million	4	6
Over $1 million	6	8
Losses	10	14

reach consensus on how to put the process into operation. The company can maintain consistency and good communication throughout the program by grouping workers into teams and organizing committees that meet regularly. Finally, various incentives (i.e., financial, peer recognition, management recognition) are of vital importance in motivating new product participants. Overall, once the company has acted on these points and redirected resources appropriately to reemphasize newness, it will be able to improve its new product program and establish competitive edge.

EXHIBIT 3.27 Key Factors for Implementing a New Product Measurement System

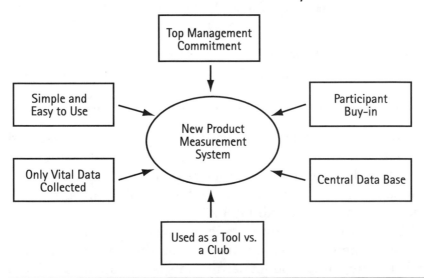

CHAPTER 4

The New
Product Blueprint

R*isk, innovation, entrepreneurship, and growth are not liberal or conservative issues. They represent an urgent national priority.*

Reprinted with permission of *Inc.* magazine, copyright© 1987, Inc. Publishing Corporation.

A new product blueprint describes the role that new products will play in satisfying the overall growth goals of a company. It should include an estimate of development expenditures and investment capital needs for at least the next three years, estimated human-resource and skill requirements, desired three-to five-year revenue targets from new products, and top management's expectations for, and commitment to, new products. In short, the new product blueprint defines the direction to take. The new product strategy describes the game plan in terms of how to get there. And the development process is the road map that outlines the path to take to reach the ultimate destination.

Armed with the results of the new product diagnostic audit, management is well equipped with information to create a new products blueprint and guide the development of a new product strategy. Internal strengths to exploit in generating new concepts have been identified, the reasons behind past new product performance are more accurately understood, and potential internal impediments can now be addressed. At this point, the key benefit from the audit is informed decision mak-

ing and judgment that can be applied to setting up the new
product blueprint and strategy. You now have a more realistic
picture of what the company can expect to achieve from new
products.

Shaping the Blueprint

The blueprint sets up management's growth expectations for
new products. A completed diagnostic audit serves as a reality
check on those expectations. There are several growth modes
for a company to pursue—not just new product development.
How a company wants to grow is often an indication of the
overall risk profile of the organization. Increasing market share
of existing products through line extensions and flankers is
certainly lower risk than entering new markets and categories
with new-to-the-company products. If you haven't thought
about them already, it is helpful to consider these approaches
to growth and determine which ones will most likely be used
by your own company. Examples include:

- ✧ Expanding market share of existing products
  through changes in marketing mix.
- ✧ Introducing existing products into new geographic markets and distribution channels.
- ✧ Expanding the overall market by developing
  new uses for existing products.
- ✧ Licensing existing technology or products to
  other manufacturers or receiving licenses from
  others.
- ✧ Developing new products internally.
- ✧ Entering into joint-venture agreements with
  other manufacturers.
- ✧ Acquiring companies or products to get into
  new businesses or to expand and bolster existing product lines.

The two most critical questions to address for the blueprint are:

1. What priority do new products play in the growth strategy of the company?
2. How do managers view the role of new products versus other growth models (i.e. acquisitions, joint ventures, licensing, and existing business expansion)?

Constructing a Framework

The new product blueprint can be compared to an architect's drawings for a new house. The architect in concert with the future owners discusses different ideas and gradually develops a vision of the new house. She takes these ideas and transforms them into sketches, which begin to give form and substance to the vision and then integrates them into a detailed blueprint that depicts how the owners want the house to look. However, the architect cannot build the house alone. A general contractor must be hired to interpret the blueprint and determine how best to segregate the tasks and coordinate the right mix of resources needed to build the house. After identifying the need for electricians, plumbers, and carpenters and hiring them, the general contractor must still work closely with the architect. He has the responsibility for getting the house built and will need to set up a schedule, timetable, and step-by-step procedure that delineates the building stages and specific duties of the subcontractors. The general contractor consistently monitors performance, tracks progress, and makes course corrections in the plan as appropriate. In effect, he develops a strategy for turning the architect's vision and resultant blueprint into a reality.

This example provides a good analogy to the new product development process. Shareholders and the board of directors in a company may be compared to the owners of the house. Top management has a vision of what is expected from new products and serves as the architect. Expectations are generated that relate to the role of new products in meeting the growth objectives of the corporation. Top management defines these expectations, which are drawn up in the form of a new product blueprint, and then hires a "general contractor," a new product manager, who takes responsibility for execution of the blueprint. The new product manager, like the contractor, assumes responsibility for translating the blueprint into a strategy, the execution process, and the action plan.

In order to determine how best to generate and screen new product ideas that will fulfill the expectations cited in the blueprint, the new product manager must break down the objectives into manageable parts, determine which functions new products will need to perform, and decide what screens should be used to identify the best ideas. Thus the general contractor's game plan is analogous to the new product manager's strategy. Subsequently, the manager decides on the steps to follow to get new products to market and also decides specific resources that will be needed to help execute the process. One individual cannot launch new products single-handedly any more than one good architect can build a house unassisted.

The new product strategy is intended to take the blueprint, interpret its meaning, and define in detail the new product growth gap, financial objectives, strategic roles, new product types, and screening criteria in light of the diagnostic audit findings.

Developing a New Product Blueprint

A new product blueprint describes the role of new products relative to a company's growth objectives and strategy. Driven by the risk posture of top management, long-term financial objectives of the corporation, and the growth strategy defining how the financial goals will be met, the blueprint states the intended role of new products in satisfying the corporate strategy. Growth targets may be reached by merely investing in and expanding the existing business or by acquiring companies, by launching internally developed new products, or through a combination of various growth modes. The essential purpose of the new product blueprint is to articulate, in writing, and place dimensions around, the role that new products are expected to play in fulfilling corporate growth objectives.

Moreover, management's vision for new products must be a part of the blueprint. The vision should include the size, type, and number of new products desired. It should be clear whether management envisions new business or product lines or just product improvements coming out of the effort. For any company, the growth expectation for new products typically falls under one of the following five categories as depicted in Exhibit 4.1.

Determining Growth Roles

The role of new products does change in most companies over time. This is an important issue that is often overlooked. Usually, a company's planning cycle occurs every twelve months. External market forces, competition, consumer preferences, and financial requirements change, and consequently, the role for new products may be altered. The paradox is that once the growth role for new products has been determined, it *cannot* change every year. Constant change is one of the major impediments to successful new product development. A company cannot keep stopping and starting the new product effort and still expect tangible results. Consistency is required because the development cycle for new products extends well beyond the twelve-month planning cycle. As a company's new product role gradually changes, information about that role must be communicated throughout the organization. Herein lies a frequent void between top management and middle management. The person at the top has forgotten to tell the rest of the troops that the role of new products has shifted.

Implicit in each growth role for new products is the risk posture of top management and its relative commitment to new products. As a result, companies that have a modest or high growth role tend to exhibit more of a charged-up, entrepreneurial, and dynamic new product culture. A certain domino effect and an interaction occur among the growth roles selected for new products, the environment created, the commitment made, and the attitudes conveyed toward new products.

EXHIBIT 4.1 Growth Roles for New Products

ZERO ROLE

For some companies, new products are not expected to play a role in the revenue or profit growth of the company. For them, acquisitions, licensing agreements, geographic expansion of existing products or services, and the like, are the chosen growth routes. As a result, any new product that surfaces internally, by accident or fluke, is evaluated on an opportunistic basis.

UPGRADE ROLE

For others, new products take a modest role in the growth process, typically exemplified through line extensions, additions, and revisions to existing products. With this role for new products, companies for the most part view them as the way to keep their existing product lines alive and competitively positioned. New products become tools to enhance the core business. Usually, new products contribute less than 10 percent of annual revenues in this type of company. Emphasis is placed on taking a proactive approach to new products but within a fairly narrow scope and framework.

MODEST GROWTH ROLE

This type of company clearly sees the role of new products as a growth mode integral to the success of the corporate strategy. A deliberate portion of the new product effort is directed at truly innovative new products, not only new to the world. However, line extensions, flankers, and other new product types are also part of the new product portfolio. New products typically account for 10 to 20 percent of this type of company's revenue stream.

HIGH GROWTH ROLE

The place to be in this type of company is in the new product area. Top management is involved, committed, and dedicated to this activity. Beyond developing a mix of new product types, this kind of company will pursue the development of new categories and lines of products that will afford the opportunity to enter totally new businesses. Often the financial contribution of new products to revenues will exceed 20 percent annually.

SURVIVAL ROLE

These companies are indeed active in new products but tend to react to competition by launching only me-too products that have slight improvements, lower cost, or different whistles and bells. Up to 5 to 10 percent of revenues may come from competitive-response new products. The major difference from the update-role companies is the reactionary approach rather than an offensive, proactive approach.

Selection of a high growth role may be more apt to generate a team of highly motivated managers. An upgrade role may stimulate a few sparks but certainly no blazing fires.

But the new product blueprint needs to contain more than just the relationship of new products to corporate growth goals. The blueprint must map out the evolution of roles over at least a five-year period. It must include information on the resource requirements that will be needed to accomplish the defined role for new products. An estimate of available capital and development dollars that will be devoted to new products is a key component of the blueprint. A new product budget must be established. But how can a company possibly know what its resource needs will be before it even identifies specific new products? That's the whole point. Successful companies establish broad benchmarks that begin to frame the order of magnitude of the new product efforts. They establish the process to guide the development of products rather than letting a series of new product projects gradually define the process.

For example, one food company with roughly $100 million in sales had been experiencing market-share losses resulting from a competitor's new product inroads. This encroachment made them turn to new products as a solution. Three years ago they developed a new product blueprint and estimated an expenditure of $6 million in development costs during the next five years and an additional $2 million in plant and equipment capital. Moreover, they even outlined the requirement for five new product people within the next two years and four additional R&D technicians. New products were viewed as playing a high growth role for the company.

While members of top management gulped when first presented with an expenditure level that represented 8 percent of current revenues, they also recognized that the new product objective was to add an incremental $20 million to $25 million in revenues. That would generate, on average, 40 to 45 percent gross margins. Only three years after the initial development of a new product blueprint and strategy, the company launched fourteen new products—two new to the world, six new to the company, and six line extensions—that today represent over $18 million in revenues and $7.3 million in incremental gross profits.

EXHIBIT 4.2 Components of a New Product Blueprint

A description of the *role* that new products will play in the overall growth plan of the company.

An estimated five-year budget that indicates the level of *development expenditures and investment capital* for the entire new product effort.

A profile of the *human resource requirements* needed.

A broad financial objective and *revenue target* for the composite of all new products launched during the planned period. This would include either a total revenue number or percentage of sales.

A description of how the role of new products *will mesh with other growth modes* that will be pursued, for example, acquisitions, licensing, strategic alliances, and contract arrangements.

An articulation of *top management's expectations for new products and its intended level of involvement*, that is, guidelines and performance benchmarks that define a successful new product development program and management's activities and type of participation in the process.

Signed by Senior Management

_____   _____

_____   _____

Creating the Blueprint

A sound new product blueprint must include all of the information shown in Exhibit 4.2.

An excellent way to visibly convey senior manager support to the blueprint is to have each executive sign it. In this way, everyone in the company knows that the senior executives are on the same page. A company example of a New Product Blueprint is portrayed in Exhibit 4.3.

EXHIBIT 4.3 Example of a New Product Blueprint

ROLE: HIGH NEW GROWTH

Internally developed new products are expected to represent 50 to 60 percent of new revenue growth; 20 percent to come from acquisitions, and 20 to 25 percent from existing businesses.

REVENUE TARGET

Corporate growth targets are to generate $150 million in incremental revenues during the next four years.

The target for new product revenues is $90 million by the beginning of year 5.

BUDGET

The new product development expense budget for the next two years will approximate $5 million for salaries, market research, prototype development, and market-testing costs.

Capital available for plant and equipment investments needed for new products cannot exceed $7.5 million. Commercialization launch costs cannot exceed 40 percent of year 2 revenue projections per new product.

HUMAN RESOURCE REQUIREMENTS BY YEAR 2

- New product director
- Four new product managers
- Two business analysts
- One market researcher
- Three laboratory technicians

INTERFACE WITH OTHER GROWTH MODES

Acquisitions will be aimed at acquiring product lines that will support or be complementary to the thrust of internally developed new products.

Licensing agreement will be limited to personalities that can be used in concert with new products developed.

TOP MANAGEMENT'S EXPECTATIONS/INVOLVEMENT

By year 3, top management expects at least ten new products launched, representing cumulative revenue potential of over $50 million within one to two years.

Management also expects a steady pipeline flow of new product concepts to be established by the end of the first year.

Top management will attend all monthly new product steering committee meetings and will approve/disapprove the new product strategy, all concepts prior to prototype development, and any capital expenditures over $100,000.

The worst type of new product blueprint is a list of new product projects. If your company has a list of projects currently underway that serves as a proxy for a new product blueprint, you should burn it at once. It is totally meaningless, distorts the objectives, focus, and level of commitment to new products, and accomplishes nothing more than generating a lot of aggravation. Many top executives proudly show off their list of new product projects. However, when the time comes to commit $1.5 million to one new product launch, the enthusiasm suddenly dissipates.

The new product blueprint is a concrete and tangible form of top management commitment. It reinforces the need for top management to lay itself on the line concerning the future role of new products. It also shakes out many clandestine skeletons that hide in top management's closets, like, "Well, it looks like a great opportunity, but we just don't have the funds to support it this quarter—or next." Then why has some ambitious manager been working day and night to develop a prototype?

The blueprint also enables the people working on new products to have some faith that all of their frustrations and anxieties are worth it. It is a form of security, offers long-term perspective, and establishes a common set of expectations. More concretely, it is a written document that indicates the importance of new products to the company and the role new products represent in shaping the company's future.

A final note on the key elements of a new product blueprint: Management should provide guidelines that define the minimum standards for a successful new product development program. In other words, in three to five years from now, what will it take for management to be able to say that they have been pleased with the way new products have been managed—that the effort was a success?

Success guidelines can be defined along a number of dimensions. Keep in mind that we are talking not about specific new product success criteria but, rather, about guidelines for judging the overall success of the new product development program.

The purpose of success guidelines is to get some feel for what top management wants to accomplish for the company with new products—the type of comment that the CEO would like to make at an annual shareholders or board meeting. CEOs who have been asked what it would take to rate their new product development programs a success three to five years from now have made comments like the following:

✧ To exceed the target of achieving 10 percent revenue growth from new products.

✧ To drop $2 million in incremental profits to the bottom line from new products regardless of the type, category, or revenue size.

✧ To demonstrate to the investment community that the company is committed to growth from new products.

✧ To launch, on average, four to five new-to-the-company products each year.

✧ To beat out our major competitor with enough new products that his head begins to spin.

✧ To get new products that will strengthen our position in the European market.

✧ To be able to commercialize just a couple of big hits to reinforce to all managers the fact that new products must be a way of life for us.

Thus identifying the one dimension most important to top management for new products to satisfy is an integral component of the new product blueprint. Another benefit is that the blueprint sharpens and clarifies management's expectations for new products. Those expectations can then be better communicated throughout an organization.

In Summary

The new product blueprint is usually drafted by the new product manager in concert with top management. Senior management must be included in the approval process to build a feeling of ownership and commitment throughout the company. While the blueprint sets the direction for all new product activities and relates the role of new products in satisfying corporate growth objectives, the new product strategy is the management tool that describes how the blueprint will be implemented.

CHAPTER **5**

The New Product Strategy

*T*here is nothing more difficult to plan, more doubtful of success, nor more dangerous to manage than the creation of a new system.

Niccolo Machiavelli, *The Prince*

The new product strategy consists of a definition of the *financial growth gap* and *financial goals* that new products are expected to meet, *strategic roles* that describe the functions that new products will perform, and *screening criteria* that serve as filters in determining which categories and new product concepts are most attractive to pursue.

Developing the Strategy

Without a new product strategy, it is difficult to know which direction to take. One idea may appear attractive to one person and not another. With a new product strategy, management can more quickly and effectively focus on the market categories, ideas, and concepts that match specific strategic roles. It enables managers to focus category identification and idea generation on agreed-upon targets, and it cuts down the screening time and prototype development costs incurred by false starts.

In short, the new product strategy defines how the growth objectives of the company will be satisfied by internally developed new products. It sets up the game plan for transforming the blueprint into market realities.

Financial Growth Gap

The financial gap for new products must be clearly identified. Without one, neither success nor progress can be measured. Resource requirements cannot be determined. The long-range business plan usually contains some optimistic "hockey-stick" graphs and charts. At least these often-lofty goals are a starting point to get the process underway. Developing realistic new product financial targets is critical. Targets that are too low tend to drag down managers' potential; targets too high create frustration and anxiety and cause the managers to lose their sense of commitment. While revenue and profit goals may be a stretch, and deliberately challenging, they should be attainable within reason. If not, this alone will be debilitating for new product participants, drive down morale, and weaken the new product foundation.

With the company's new product performance record in hand, senior management can develop a financial growth gap to see if their revenue target, set up in the initial blueprint, is still attainable. Again, the purpose of identifying the new product growth gap is to determine the portion of financial growth expected to come from new products. Using the information from the diagnostic audit to formulate the growth gap will provide an even better understanding of program requirements. In turn, you can accomplish resource allocation more effectively. The starting point for determining the growth gap is to examine the past revenue and profit growth of the existing core business. Then figure the total revenues and profits that new products are expected to contribute to a company's growth during a specific time period—usually three to five years.

Take, for example, a microwave-container business that has $250 million in sales and generates $18.7 million in profits. Looking back five years, the company had $125 million in sales and $7.5 million in profits. Thus, during the past five years, on average, the company has enjoyed a compound annual growth rate (CAGR) of +15 percent a year in revenue growth and +20 percent a year in profit growth.

With this historical perspective in mind, the next issues to address are as follows:

✧ Which internal and external factors will alter this growth rate during the next five years?

✧ Is competition intensifying?

✧ Are prices going up or down?

✧ Are there new competitors entering the category?

✧ Will consumer demand continue to grow at historical levels?

✧ The key question to be answered is: What is the projected growth rate of the total market category during the next five years?

The reason this question is so essential is that it provides a benchmark to measure a specific company's growth projections. If a category is forecast to grow at 8 percent a year, and a company is projecting a 25 percent annual growth rate for a specific product line in that category, management may be filled with delusions of grandeur. However, if the company is planning to take a price reduction, substantially increase its advertising budget, expand its distribution base, or the like, then a 25 percent growth rate for the company may be feasible.

A five-year financial growth gap can be developed by building up the revenue projections estimated from each growth mode. Determine for your own company what percentage of future growth is expected to come from each source. (See Exhibit 5.1.)

Now percentages or absolute revenue dollar projections can be applied to each growth mode. This framework will begin to calibrate the relative degree of importance of new products to alternative growth routes.

For example, take a power-instruments consumer-durables company that currently does $500 million in sales and has been growing at an 8 percent compound annual growth rate

---

EXHIBIT 5.1 Sources (by Percentage) of Revenue Growth or Forecast Revenues

- Existing businesses and product lines
- New product line additions, revisions, and extensions to existing products
- New-to-the-company and new-to-the-world products
- Acquisitions and joint ventures
- Other growth modes, for example, licensing, alliances with other companies, minority investments

---

during the past five years. The projection for the future is a 6 percent growth rate, resulting in a revenue projection of $1.05 billion in five years. The only breakdown in the long-range plan is between existing and new products, jointly estimated to generate $900 million, and acquisitions forecast to contribute the remaining $150 million. The objective, of course, is to break out the $900 million into components that will be meaningful in framing the new product effort.

In examining the existing business, the product lines can be grouped into three product categories: power instruments, lighting products, and small appliances. Each of the groups has grown at 6 percent, 12 percent, and 3 percent, respectively, during the past five years. Power instruments and small appliances, in particular, have been under intense foreign competition. Higher-value new products are defined in the plan as a key way to counteract foreign competitors. Power instruments' existing business is forecast to grow at 8 percent annually and small appliances' by 5 percent. Lighting products, on the other hand, are expected to grow 18 percent annually. Sales increases have to come through geographic penetration, product differentiation, and some price increases. Apparently, this business is well positioned for future growth.

What are the financial growth expectations for new products? First, let's determine the revenue contribution to come from the existing business. Based on the forecast growth-rate projections, the current $500 million is expected to grow to $766 million, representing a 9 percent annual increase. (See Exhibit 5.2.)

EXHIBIT 5.2 Financial Growth Expectations Example

	Current Product Size ($Million)	Growth Rate	Five-Year Projection ($Million)
Power instruments	$225	8%	$ 330
Lighting	$ 85	18%	$ 194
Small Appliances	$190	5%	$ 242
Revenues from existing products	$500	9%	$ 766
Forecast revenues from new products			$ 134
Acquisitions			$ 150
Total	$500	16%	$1,050

At this point, we know that the remaining $134 million is expected to come from products that are not currently in the marketplace. Within five years, these products will represent roughly 13 percent of the total $1,050 million revenue base. This suggests that from a financial standpoint the role of new products falls into the modest-growth-role category since the revenue-contribution expectation falls within the 10 to 20 percent range. Most important, it begins to shape the magnitude of effort that will be required to develop more than $25 million worth of new products, on average, annually.

The next step is to break out the $134 million by new product types into a realistic cut between line extensions and new-to-the-company products in either related or unrelated businesses. Exhibit 5.3 shows that the growth gap for new products is about equally balanced between new products (extensions) that will support and expand the existing businesses and new products (new to company) that will catapult the company into new businesses.

Exhibit 5.4 shows the company's $134 million growth gap for new products and other sources of growth. Nearly 13 percent of the company's revenues in five years from now are expected to come from internally developed new products.

One of the useful things that can come from growth gap

EXHIBIT 5.3 New Product Types

New product line extensions
(Including revisions and additions)

Power instruments	$ 20 million
Lighting	$ 15 million
Small appliances	$ 30 million
Subtotal	$ 65 million
New-to-the company products	$ 69 million
Total new products	$ 134 million

analysis is the identification of a range of financial and nonfinancial issues that relate back to the blueprint and help set the direction. For example, the implications for this company include the following:

- ✧ The new product and acquisition expectations are roughly evenly balanced. The company wants to add $150 million from acquisitions and $134 million from new products.
- ✧ The mix of line extensions and additions versus new-to-the-company products is also relatively balanced.

To develop this mix of new products, it is likely that the company will need to hire a full-time new product manager. A separate new product department, team, or division may be needed for the new-to-the-company products, while line extensions might be managed by current product managers. If the balance is totally skewed to line extensions and additions, the new product effort might best be carried out by existing business marketing managers. Moreover, a heavier R&D budget may also be needed to support the new-to-the-company product efforts.

Total development costs and profit expectations will be higher, and, consequently, the overall new product effort will

EXHIBIT 5.4 Defining the New Products Revenue Growth Gap

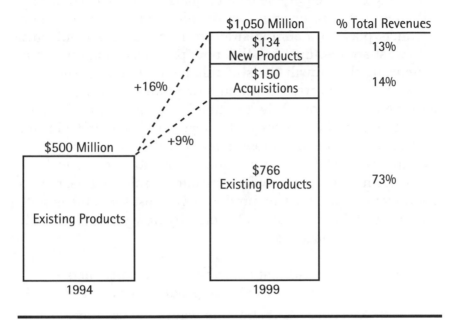

have a higher risk, since new-to-the-company products represent one-half of the new product effort.

Management must recognize that new product revenues will not begin flowing in for at least one to two years. (Development time is often overlooked in setting new product targets.) Thus the $134 million in sales from new products, in effect, are expected to be generated within a three- to four-year period. This may be an overly optimistic goal. The company wants to more than double its size within five years. With 27 percent of total revenues coming from new products and acquisitions, a high degree of focused attention and dedicated resources will be required to achieve these goals. The assumption should be that a new product team is already in the works or one will soon be underway.

The financial growth gap helps to break down and better define the new product targets. It is a way to provide a reality check on the new products objectives and begins to provide a framework for considering financial and human resource requirements.

Strategic Roles

New product strategic roles are largely based on a company's specific growth requirements and goals. That is, beyond contributing to future revenues and profits, what roles will new products play? In defining strategic roles, management must ask, what are the functions that new products should serve in supporting the growth goals of this company? Strategic roles help pinpoint the areas in which new products are expected to perform to either build the existing business or take the company into new businesses and categories. Each strategic role should fulfill a business requirement, whether it is to bolster existing product lines or provide a way to enter new businesses or markets. Both types of strategic roles are geared toward identifying how new products will best serve the growth objectives of the corporation. We classify new product strategic roles into two categories:

- ✧ Requisite roles that describe how new products will help grow the existing product or business.
- ✧ Expansive roles that define ways new products can get a company into totally new businesses, markets, or consumer segments.

There is often a high degree of overlap between requisite and expansive roles. What's important is that new product roles be developed to define what a company expects new products to do beyond increasing revenues and profits. No single role stands as a touchstone; successful companies have used a variety of new product types to satisfy a wide range of roles. Often a new-to-the-world or new-to-the-company product will satisfy expansive roles, whereas line extensions, repositioning, improvements, and cost reductions will be used to fulfill requisite roles. However, each new product type can potentially meet any role.

Requisite roles are usually geared toward defending or protecting a business from competition, supporting or expanding the existing business, or applying an internal strength, such as a new technology or raw material cost advantage. In addition, requisite roles may be aimed at solving existing business problems; for example, utilizing excess capacity or waste by-products, offsetting seasonal fluctuations in sales, or improving manufacturing costs.

Expansive roles describe ways that new products can move a company into a new category, market, or business. It may represent a more significant investment than new products that serve requisite roles, but the returns also are usually greater. Expansive roles may include entering a new foreign country, establishing a foothold in a product category targeted to the elderly segment, or getting into the automotive aftermarket—a new category for the company with a series of new products.

To understand what new product roles are supposed to do for a company, they need to be examined from an internal perspective—in terms of the business requirements they will fulfill, not just the external consumer needs they will satisfy. Granted, the overriding compelling driver behind any successful new product is the ability of that product to perform better than any alternative product available in meeting a consumer's need. However, taken a given need, new products are not created equal for all companies. Consequently, companies launching similar products will most likely end up with varying degrees of success in terms of product quality, consumer acceptance, and market performance. There are four reasons why this frequently occurs:

1. The new product did not draw upon the company's internal strengths.
2. The new product did not have clearly defined objectives or roles tied to the overall business objectives of the company.
3. Insufficient resources were committed to the product during the development process.
4. Execution of the product's launch was poorly performed, coordinated, or timed.

By determining corporate growth objectives and strategic requirements, a company can develop new product strategic roles aimed at serving specific functions that will address the company's overall growth requirements. A company is then positioned to manage its new product portfolio with the same degree of certainty and calibrated risk with which it manages the existing business portfolio. A single new product may satisfy several strategic roles. For example, Quaker Oats' launch of rice cakes may have satisfied both requisite and expansive roles. It allowed the company to enter the low calorie segment of the snack food business, and it expanded the existing snack business into more healthful foods, exploited the equity of the Quaker Oats brand name in grain based foods, capitalized on the channel clout from the direct sales force, and increased the total share of shelf space in retail outlets. On the other hand, several different new product types may be required to satisfy just one strategic role.

An example of satisfying expansive roles is illustrated by Kodak's launch of lithium-powered batteries called Ultralife, which last twice as long as batteries with alkaline cells. This product satisfied an opportunistic role by enabling Kodak to penetrate the battery market. But it also serves an expansive role for Black & Decker, since that company began to design household items ranging from flashlights to smoke detectors using Kodak's batteries.

For a soap and detergent manufacturer, new products that protected its share of shelf space would represent a requisite role. A laundry detergent that softened fabric and controlled static could increase the company's shelf space and might deter a competitor from creeping up. In contrast, the same company might set up an expansive new product role enabling it to get into a totally new segment of the home laundry market, for example, dry cleaning. In this case, a new product line that allowed consumers to dry clean their clothes at home would satisfy a more expansive role. Dryel is a new brand launched in 1999 that offers home dry-cleaning. For Procter & Gamble, this is a good example of an expansive role, which goes beyond their existing business.

Minnetonka's introduction of Softsoap, a perceived new-to-the-world product for in-home consumer use, even

---

Exhibit 5.5 Different Strategic Roles for Similar Products

Requisite	*Keebler*	*Pillsbury*
	Soft Batch Cookies	All Ready Pie Crust
Expansive	*Keebler*	*Procter & Gamble*
	Ready Crust Pie Crust	Duncan Hines Chocolate Chip Cookies

---

though liquid soap had existed for years in public restrooms, can be viewed as a product that satisfied an expansive role. Preempting competition and securing a strong market share initially in a new soap category led this company into the bathroom and the kitchen. Here was a tiny Midwest company up against giants and soaring ahead of them for a while. Imagine the chagrin at Procter & Gamble and Lever Brothers.

Occasionally, a type of new product that satisfies a requisite role for one company fulfills an expansive role for another. This is simply because companies have different resource bases, market needs, and strengths and weaknesses. They look at the same product category with different eyes, different needs, different expectations—all of which will influence their approaches to new product development. The focus comes from the internal perspective of the company. To illustrate, let's examine four new products launched by Keebler, Pillsbury, and Procter & Gamble in two product categories. (See Exhibit 5.5.)

Keebler's introduction of Soft Batch Cookies satisfied a requisite role, largely a defensive move directed at protecting its retail market share. Nabisco and Frito-Lay had introduced chocolate chip cookies offering more chips, different texture, and a "more fresh-baked taste," intensifying the pressure on Keebler's shelf space. In contrast to this requisite role, Procter & Gamble's entry into the chocolate chip cookie market, under the Duncan Hines brand name, satisfied an expansive, market-driven role. It wanted to gain a new position in a growing snack-food niche, outside its existing cake-mix base, driven heavily by advertising and brand name identification.

Keebler's Ready-Crust piecrusts, on the other hand, served an expansive role by enabling the company to expand into new dessert-related, convenience-oriented product categories where the company had no presence. Yet Pillsbury's piecrust entrant satisfied a requisite role; it was primarily developed to expand shelf exposure at retail and utilize excess flour. Thus, depending upon the internal perspective of a company, new products can satisfy either requisite or expansive roles, or both. These roles are often driven by internal, market, or expansion requirements.

An important observation is that these products were not developed merely to fill a predetermined revenue gap. Rather, they all satisfied a strategic business requirement first and served as an incremental source of revenue and profit second. Many companies tend to drive their entire new product activity toward meeting financial targets rather than satisfying strategic roles. Hence, they miss many opportunities for bolstering their core businesses through new products. In the process of building on strategic role considerations, a company should enhance the potential for above average financial returns and lower the risk.

Let's look at one more company to see how roles can be used. A candy company in the Midwest had three key corporate growth roles: (1) to increase its nominal sales revenues by 15 percent, (2) to maintain existing profit margins, and (3) to realize 70 percent of projected growth from existing products and 30 percent from new products. Top management decided that to achieve these goals, its corporate strategic objectives had to focus on building its U.S. market share and entering new foreign markets. The question then became: How can new products best help to meet these objectives?

For this candy manufacturer to build market share in the U.S., new products could have played several roles: defended the company's competitive position in the marketplace, protected current share of shelf space, or capitalized on the company's existing distribution system. Management developed new-to-the-world products and new product lines to encourage brand switching and stimulate consumer demand as a means of defending its competitive posture. Moreover, they also developed line extensions and flavor flankers to protect current shelf space. All four types of new products were used to satisfy strategic roles that met the goals of the company.

It is evident, then, that both requisite and expansive roles are closely tied to internal strengths. Expansive roles, however, are driven largely by external market opportunities, while requisite roles spring directly from a company's existing competitive advantages.

Linking the Diagnostic Audit to the New Product Strategy

To illustrate the process of linking a diagnostic audit with the development of strategic roles, let's look at a consumer-non-durables company with a strong share position in the household-tool category.

The company enjoys a 25 percent dollar market share. The company has had a steady revenue growth of 18 percent annually during the last five years, but encroaching foreign competition, coupled with the growing risk of dependency on virtually one supplier, makes management realize that a rigorous and disciplined new products planning process is necessary to protect future margins and growth.

As a result, the company conducted a thorough new products diagnostic audit. Among its findings, it learned that over the last five years, the company had generated $10 million from new products. A good record, but one that fell far short of competition. Numerous ideas not related to tools but aimed at the do-it-yourself market had been floating around without direction. Many good opportunities had been lost because this market had not been targeted by the company. Yet people had been working on these ideas anyway. In addition, an unwritten requisite goal, reducing dependency on one supplier through new products, had not been met, and furthermore, dependence had increased. Also included in this self-assessment were those internal strengths the company could bring to bear in its new product program. An examination of technologies and patents owned, manufacturing and marketing advantages relative to competition, and competitive market analysis revealed five areas where the company had a competitive edge upon which to build its new products program.

- ✧ *Cost/Scale Advantage*—Even though a major raw material was purchased solely from one overseas supplier, the company enjoyed significant unit-cost advantages through scale economies. The business was volume-sensitive, and the company's leading market-share position provided economic cost leverage. Moreover, increasing volume throughput, in tandem with processing improvements, would result in even further cost benefits to the company.

- ✧ *Technology*—The company's existing CAD/CAM design capabilities were truly state of the art. They offered precision in tooling and cost-effective development of new products from the drawing board to finished prototype. Moreover, the company had several product and process patents pending that could provide some big-hit opportunities.

- ✧ *Distribution and Sales Coverage*—With current distribution in hardware stores, mass merchandisers, do-it-yourself stores, and a wide mix of specialty-tool stores, the company was well positioned to launch additional new products in existing channels. The sales force had established strong trade relationships with sales reps and buyers. It was always running well-received contests for these customers. These factors, combined with brand-name equity, meant that gaining shelf space on new products in these channels would be relatively easy.

- ✧ *Consumer Position and Brand-Name Equity*— Consumer perception of product quality was extremely high. Competitors did not enjoy the same high standing in perceived quality or brand-name recognition. The company had spent heavy advertising dollars to bolster high quality brand-name awareness. It was feasible that this brand-name equity would be transferable to new products. In fact, its brand name alone would communicate quality to consumers even before they understood the new products' specific benefits.

✧ *Entrepreneurial Environment and Committed Management*—Management was willing to take the risks associated with moving out of the existing core-products base. Over $20 million had been allocated to developing new products during the next two years. Venture teams were established that consisted of some of the top talent across functions within the company.

High margins generated through premium-priced products and a strong cash/growth balance in managing assets led the company to set aggressive growth targets for the future. The company had developed a new product blueprint that was linked to its corporate plan. It identified five major strategic goals to be satisfied through its future new products:

1. Achieve a 20 percent increase in dollar market share from existing and new products.
2. Generate $50 million from new-to-the-world products not yet in the marketplace.
3. Diversify into do-it-yourself product categories besides tools.
4. Expand tools distribution to the West Coast market in do-it-yourself retail outlets through existing and new products.
5. Reduce dependency on one source of supply.

The company had developed several basic requisite and expansive strategic roles to guide its growth. It determined that first it must protect its existing business to maintain its current clout in the market. Several requisite roles were formulated to protect and expand this business by capitalizing on internal strengths. They ranged from increasing market share to developing lower-cost tools, utilizing new supply sources to compete with foreign competitors through the development of new products.

Expansive roles, such as exploiting existing technology and entering new do-it-yourself retail niches in the U.S. market, were developed to launch the company into new product lines and new business categories.

The next step was to calibrate the relative degree of risk for each new product associated with specific strategic roles. To assess the risk for each strategic role, management developed a weighting system based on the company's internal strengths. The leverage of each internal strength was valued, and the weights indicated the degree of importance a particular strength had in contributing to strategic roles. The requisite and expansive roles were then ranked in order of relative importance to the business objectives, and performance criteria were developed based on the assigned risk factors. The lowest risk is associated with a cost reduction that is intended to play the role of securing a dominant market share and compete more effectively with foreign competitors. The highest risk is attached to a new-to-the-world product designed to establish a foothold in a new geographic market.

Yet the findings from the diagnostic audit proved instrumental in getting the whole new product project off to the right start. In a sense, it provided a foundation for the architect and contractor. They clearly saw that to meet these challenges (especially with respect to generating an additional $50 million), they needed a separate new product team, *written* plans, and clear accountability.

Separating the "can do" from the "would like to do" involves measuring the relative degree of risk of each potential new product matched to strategic roles. Strategic roles provide direction for building a company with internally developed new products. The roles also provide a way for top management to offer input on the direction of the new product efforts without getting involved in the nitty-gritty stages of development. As you can also see, new product strategic roles link the entire development process to corporate growth and financial objectives. With increased planning and commitment early in the new product direction-setting process, companies can remove a good deal of uncertainty and really manage new product development.

Screening Criteria

Screening criteria should be developed in order to set priorities on market categories and new product concepts. By setting screening criteria to measure the attractiveness of new product concepts, a company increases its chances for new product success. While most companies tend to use sales revenues, profit contribution, and return on invested capital for screening a new concept, other financial criteria may be even more appropriate, such as margins, payback, and return on sales or assets. Regardless of the specific performance measures chosen, successful companies identify a common basis for agreeing on screening criteria and then stick to them—for each new concept under consideration. Strategic roles and new product types must also be linked to financial-screening criteria. As one new product director for a consumer durables company noted, "First, strategic objectives are set, and then we establish screens that differ by role and new product type."

For example, the Toro Company uses several techniques to generate new product ideas and calibrate risk. What business objective should new products satisfy? Their snow products and lighting businesses may have resulted from these strategic roles: Utilize off-season capacity and offset sales cyclically.

Identifying a simple direction can often provide successful new product results. That is because managers are united. They share a common, focused direction—one that can be interpreted differently but one that keeps new product players working toward a commonly agreed-upon set of objectives.

Beyond establishing strategic roles, Toro well understands and utilizes screening criteria to filter out the less attractive opportunities and concentrates on higher potential-return ventures. The first type of screen Toro uses is a comparison of each new product concept under examination with the corporate mission statement for new products, their blueprint. To paraphrase the mission statement for their Consumer Products Division, Toro wants new products to be outdoor, gas-powered, maintenance-related equipment. Quality and pricing must communicate upscale and premium price/value. No "cheap" products are allowed.

This mission statement in and of itself represents a fine-meshed sieve for screening new product ideas. If a concept is not an outdoor machine that helps the consumer with some type of chore, then it probably won't pass to the next stage of development. This is an extremely cost-effective screen. Whether it is too fine meshed is always open for discussion. But the point is, a lot of time will not be wasted nor dollars spent on concepts that wander into areas that will never receive top management support and financial commitment.

After a concept passes the Toro corporate mission screen, it then has to pass a quantitative screen on potential sales revenues and profits. A minimum sales- and gross-margin threshold has been established that every new product must satisfy. Subsequent to satisfying the minimum financial criteria, in-depth business analysis is conducted on the concept to determine the following:

✧ Who will buy it? What is the market potential and who are the target customers?

✧ Why will the customer buy it? How is it different from competitive offerings?

✧ Is the product unique? Does it truly have superior benefits?

✧ Does the innovation yield a product that will allow the customer to do the task better than ever before?

If the concept passes through the business-analysis screen then it is placed in the formal new product development process. At this point, additional competitive analysis is undertaken to pinpoint the desired product characteristics. Management does recognize the need for the process to be flexible at times, given competitive new product entrants, and will occasionally alter the step-by-step stages in the process.

The purpose of screening criteria, therefore, is to provide a consistent way, with limited management emotion and bias, to compare new product opportunities against one another. If companies had unlimited funds and resources, there would be no need at all for screening criteria and performance benchmarks. A company would just launch every new idea it came up with. That not being the case, companies must make tradeoffs and choose those opportunities that offer the highest utilization of scarce resources. Screening criteria, then, become the common language that can be spoken by new product managers and top management.

While you can force any new concept to fit established screening criteria by changing the market, cost, consumer demand, or competitive assumptions, at least the ground rules are understood and can be used to test the underlying assumptions that are being made. Companies use screening criteria to prioritize categories and new ideas and concepts. The purpose of screens is to enable managers to compare one opportunity with another to determine which ones potentially offer the best fit to the company's objectives, internal strengths, and return requirements. Screening criteria are usually applied at three stages of the execution process: (1) setting priorities for category selection, (2) concept development, and (3) after-business analysis. Exhibit 5.6 shows the relationship of screening criteria to these steps in the new product process.

The potential danger of screening criteria, and the reason many new product managers shy away from them, is that these managers have been burned by top management too often when the performance of the product in the marketplace did not perform as expected. It is much "safer" for one's career to base personal performance evaluations on objectives—for instance, to launch five new products each year or develop products that will provide a new business opportunity to the company. These kinds of meaningless objectives are usually achieved. However, it takes a totally different risk posture to be held accountable for generating an incremental $50 million in revenues and $4 million in profits from products currently not on the market. Consequently, top management must set an appropriate tone and foster a supportive environment that allows mistakes to be made in the new product area. Likewise, new product managers need to be willing to take some risks.

EXHIBIT 5.6 How Screening Criteria Fit Into Overall Process

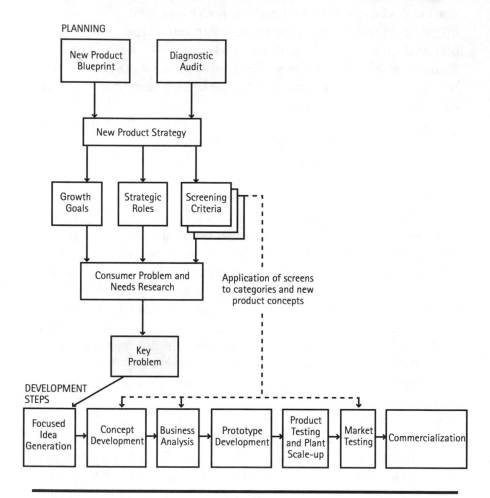

In Summary

All too often, companies want to overlook the material presented in these past chapters. Rather, they want to skip the pre-
liminaries and start: "Just tell me how to develop new
products—what are the steps I need to set up to get new products out the door?" However, the development process itself is
virtually worthless unless adequate time and energy have been
expended up front in shaping the direction for new products.

The new product strategy, therefore, is the vital link that companies need to translate corporate goals into new product realities. The strategy enables a company to work from the inside out—first to focus on internal strengths, strategic roles, and screens, and then move outside to understand potential consumer needs, identify attractive categories, and generate new product concepts. More and more, best practice companies are improving the effectiveness of their new product dollars by spending the time initially in planning for future new product investments.

Well-defined strategic roles provide the link between the product itself and the growth objectives of the company. They are derived from the strategic business requirements of the company. The determination of business requirements depends largely upon a company's growth needs. In conjunction with the findings from a diagnostic audit, the development of a well-defined new product strategy also sets the stage for developing screening criteria to accelerate the new product development process. This in turn helps reduce the risks associated with new product activities.

Our first P (Plan) of the MAP System™ is presented in Chapters 3, 4, and 5. The Diagnostic Audit, The New Product Blueprint and The New Product Strategy are the key elements of this critical upfront innovation step—planning.

The Process

The second P (Process) of the MAP System™ is presented in the next two chapters. The first chapter describes the role that screening criteria can play to help diversify risk, and the next one explains how to institutionalize a systematic, step-wise development process. A commonly understood process with agreed-upon screening criteria sets up the "machinery" to ensure a full pipeline and steady stream of new products is in place to fuel the company's growth engine.

In my three-day executive course ("New Product Development for Strategic Competitive Advantage") at the Kellogg Graduate School of Business, one of the questions I ask each group of sixty executives is: "What is the #1 barrier or obstacle to new product success within your organization?" With uncanny consistency, the answer that always seems to surface in one form or another is: lack of risk-taking. This section shows how the Process makes risk-taking manageable and productive.

6

Assessing and Managing Risk

I n the area of new product development, R&D-
driven companies have traditionally been rather
disconnected from the underlying needs of their
marketplace. . . . Companies often become blindly
enamored by their novel technology and then can't
understand why the world doesn't beat a path to
their door to purchase it. The answer is obvious: a
technology is valuable only when it is relevant to
the marketplace.

Richard Strezo, Principal, Kuczmarski & Associates, in *Chemical
Market Reporter* (January 19, 1999). p. 1.

In most companies, people fear taking risks. They are afraid of
failure, losing their job, losing their status, or negatively im-
pacting their career and compensation. The irony is that senior
management usually expresses the opposite. "I wish my people would step out of the box, take some risks, and expand
their thinking into new areas, "explains a CEO of a $2 billion
chemical company.

Obviously, we need to change the risk-averse mindset that
permeates most large corporations today. Internet IPOs have
clearly demonstrated how a risk-taking, quick response, and
culturally passionate group of people can successfully launch
a totally new-to-the-world business. Amazon.com, e-Bay, Ask
Jeeves, and Redhat didn't even exist just a couple of years ago.

Using Screening Criteria to Calibrate Risk

Screening criteria can help mitigate risk. By getting management to agree upfront on the parameters that will be accepted, a new products team should feel "safe, " secure, and confident in understanding the game rules. If a new product passes the screens, then the team should be willing to assume greater risk.

The purpose of screens is to help, not hurt, the new product development process. Screens help to clarify whether or not a new product concept should move to the next step of the development process. Of course, screening criteria does not guarantee new product success in the marketplace, but they do increase the probabilities of success and help to yield higher hit rates of commercialized new products overall.

Risk is the difference between expected return and required investment. As the variance widens between expected return and investment, the risk increases. As the variance narrows the risk decreases. But the fallacy is to simply follow the path of perceived "lower risk." Lower-risk projects mean lower returns. While the risk or probability of failure is greater with totally new innovations, the concomitant return potential is also significantly higher.

The simple answer to managing risk in new products is to diversify. Diversify by new product types, diversify by satisfying different strategic roles, diversify by developing new products for different market categories and businesses.

Thinking about new products as a stock portfolio is a good analogy. A diversified portfolio will include some blue chips, large caps, small caps, consistent dividend providers, IPOs, and high growth stocks. Overtime, the objective is for the total portfolio to grow at an acceptable rate. Every year, some portion of the stocks won't clear this hurdle, but others will far exceed it.

The same is true for new products. Consider a portfolio that includes new-to-the-world and new-to-the-company along with line extensions, upgrades, feature enhancements, and product improvements. Blending breakthrough new products with "me-toos" and "better-thans," spreads risk. Consequently, best practice companies create a balanced portfolio of high and low risk-and-return new products.

As discussed earlier, once the strategic roles have been developed to guide new product concepts, screening criteria must be developed from these strategic roles to "validate" new product concepts and ventures. Screening criteria force management to examine a new product idea against a number of specific parameters before any investments are made. This works as a safeguard against shooting from the hip—it reinforces the need for sound business analysis. Use of screening criteria can reduce the number of new product failures, which affect not only the earnings of the company, but also the morale of management and the sales force. So as you can guess, using the criteria reduces the level of risk associated with new products.

The underlying question to be answered when analyzing risk is, how much are you willing to stake for a certain level of return? And that question itself is complicated. Many factors affect it, as the following example illustrates.

A veteran gambler in Monte Carlo may be willing to bet only 20,000 francs at baccarat since he knows the house has the odds in that game. On the other hand, he may bet 100,000 francs at blackjack since he can count the cards and therefore has a slight edge over the house. Finally, he may end up investing 500,000 francs in the Grand Prix because he used to race cars himself, knows all of the cars and drivers, and won the last two years. The last bet has the lowest risk for *him*.

However, in the following year we suddenly see that the Great Gamblino has totally changed his betting strategy. Why? Because external factors have changed, and therefore he has shaped a new game plan. He now knows the baccarat dealer and has a substantial edge over the house—cheating. His baccarat bets have increased fivefold to 100,000 francs. He also knows that the roulette wheel and the house favor red, so he's up to 50,000 francs for each of these bets. However, for the Grand Prix, he's betting only 10,000 francs. Most of the drivers have changed and he doesn't know anything about them this year. So he decides to risk only a small amount on the Grand Prix. Our gambler has established betting criteria to determine how he will risk his money. In the new product arena, these criteria are considered screens.

Every opportunity must be evaluated and passed through screens as internal and external factors change. A concept that didn't make it a year ago may now pass quickly through the screening criteria. It's not that the criteria changed, but rather that the assumptions about the opportunity changed.

So by establishing a consistent set of screens, managers have a way to calibrate the relative risk of any concept—even ones previously rejected—and change or hedge their bets. As already mentioned, screening criteria *can* be used as a tool or club, but the only effective way to use screens is as tools to assist managers in setting priorities on opportunities, balancing the overall new product risk, and better allocating resources.

Most companies tend to define themselves as either new product innovators or new product followers. The *innovators* establish competitive new product leadership by building on technological advantages, undertaking preemptive marketing strategies, and investing heavily in the development and launch of new products. The *followers*, however, maintain a low-risk profile, and react to competition by generating "second, but better" new products. Either or both of these approaches can provide successful new product results. One is not necessarily better than the other, but neither approach provides a practical direction for the role new products should play in meeting corporate growth roles.

Innovation requires risk taking and funding to back it. Once an "innovator" culture has been established, the worst thing possible is to jerk the team back into a "follower" mode. It is essential to clearly define which camp a company wants to be in and then follow that specific direction for as long as possible.

Risk and Selecting New Product Types

A company must examine the types of new products they want to pursue that that will satisfy the company's strategic roles and accommodate its risk profile. As shown in Exhibit 6.1,

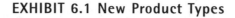

EXHIBIT 6.1 New Product Types

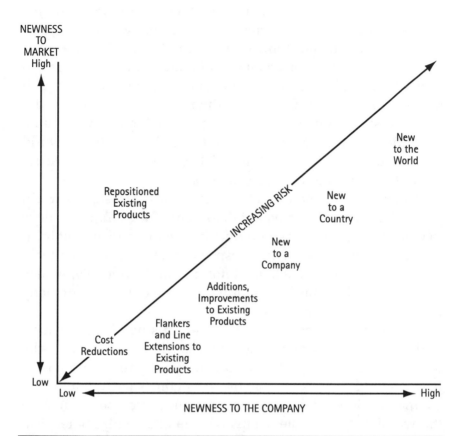

each new product type can be defined according to its relative degree of newness to the company and perceived level of newness to consumers. As would be expected, new-to-the-world products enjoy the highest degree of newness to both a company and consumers. In contrast, an improvement to an existing product may not even be perceived as a change by consumers. The result is that as the degree of product newness increases from low to high (along either measure), the relative riskiness of the new product increases. In addition, there is usually a correlation between the risk line and new product types. Usually, the highest development cost comes with a new-to-the-world product; the lowest with a line extension.

As the relative degree of *newness* increases for both the company and consumers, the degree of risk for that new product type escalates. Thus, if a company chooses to pursue nothing but new-to-the-world and new-to-the company product types, the new product portfolio is a high-risk one. On the other hand, if a company spreads its mix of new products across different types of new products, the risk is better balanced, and chances for a successful new product program are enhanced.

Successful companies tend to balance their new product portfolio. They go after the higher big-hit, new-to-the-world opportunities along with lower-risk line extensions, cost reductions, and product improvements.

Companies are more likely to develop a new-to-the-world product than any other type if the intent of the strategic role is to maintain a position as a product innovator or to exploit technology in a new way. This is especially evident in high-technology companies, such as information technology, where advances in electronics have prompted the outgrowth of many new-to-the-world products.

Managers often lose sight of the return side of the equation with higher-risk new product types. They succumb to the lower-risk, me-too syndrome. But in examining hundreds of new products across companies, it is consistently found that companies' most successful new products are usually new to the world or new to the company—the ones with higher risk. At the same time, many companies' biggest failures also fall into these two new product category types. But the fact remains that unless risk taking is woven into the fabric of a new product organization, the upside returns from new products will be limited. "No pain, no gain" is a fitting adage.

Manipulating New Product Risk

New-to-the-world products or new-to-the-company product lines typically have a higher risk than, say, cost reductions or repositioning. However, the relative risks involved with each new product type are not unalterable—a company's previous experience with various new product types can change the relative risk of each type for that company. Risk can be manipulated in the following ways:

- ✧ Develop a portfolio of new products that cut across different types and varying levels of risk.
- ✧ Draw upon internal strengths and past new product experience.
- ✧ Increase the number of launches; the more attempts, the higher the probability for success becomes.
- ✧ Define and agree upon the internal new product direction.

With truly innovative new products, there is a greater variability of return and outcome. But big risk often brings big profit. New-to-the-world and new-to-the company products most often provide companies with the big hits. While they frequently represent the fewest number of launches, they have the greatest potential for return.

New product development is often separated from current business operations (or product development) is because of the associated risk of new products. Moreover, company compensation systems are geared to risk aversion: new product development and product management don't mesh if one is trying to stimulate risk-taking in new products and the other is encouraging margin maintenance in existing products. If managers are given responsibility for existing products as well as new products, they will concentrate their time and attention on the existing line since the risk is lower and the probability of their investment outcome is more certain.

Manipulating the new product portfolio is a key risk-reducing action step. Combining different levels of risk into the new product plan makes the overall risk of the program lower than it would be for any single given individual new product. The chances of success for the overall new product effort are far greater than probability of success of any one new product. Diversification can reduce risk, and screening criteria serve as the filters to further reduce that risk. But let's not forget the role that company experience and internal strengths have in assessing risk. These two factors probably represent the most valuable risk-reducing valve that any company has. A firm's functional and new product experience, as well as its comfort level in making the required investment, influence the relative riskiness of the new product type. Consider two companies, each evaluating the same two new product opportunities. The first opportunity is a new-to-the-world product; the second is a new product line. Company A has a higher level of experience in developing new product lines and good technical background for both products but little experience in the level of investment required for the new-to-the-world opportunity. For this company, the new-to-the-company product is more attractive as evidenced by a higher expected return.

Company B, however, has a higher level of experience in developing new-to-the-world products and has a poor manufacturing base for the new product line opportunity. This company does have the experience and comfort level in making major investments—especially in the range required for this new-to-the-world opportunity. For this company, the new-to-the-world product is more attractive.

Why are new-to-the-world products usually fraught with higher risk? Because these products often lack information concerning consumer attitudes, purchasing behavior, usage, and the like. After all, if a company already has a product in the market against which another company proposes a new-to-the-company product, the second company can determine consumer reactions, purchase frequency, and attitudes toward use, and make the appropriate changes to be more competitive. When dealing with a new-to-the-world product, those data do not exist.

For innovative products that require a change in consumer behavior, risk is high because consumers must be educated, and it is difficult to assess whether the education will have the desired effect. New-to-the-world products diffuse slowly through the population, because they often require a change in values and habits. While new-to-the-world products fill consumer needs, the consumer may not have the ability to understand or the willingness to acknowledge the product benefit or advantage. Likewise, high investment spending is required to support the launch of a new-to-the-world product; reinforcement and repetition of message and consumer education are needed to change behavior patterns, and that's costly. (See Exhibit 6.2.)

Companies must take the risk of developing innovative products. The payout is too great to let potential hits go by. Granted, the downside is a lot less for the line extensions and me-toos, but so is the upside. Of course, truly innovative products demand more time, resources, and money—the three variables most cherished by corporate management. Well, the old adage, "You get what you pay for," is applicable to the new product game.

EXHIBIT 6.2 Examples of Innovative New Products

DEGREE ANTIPERSPIRANT

Helene Curtis' Degree was the first major breakthrough product in the antiperspirant market in nearly a decade. While it took five years to develop, Helene Curtis achieved immediate market success by establishing number four market-share position in the category in less than one year.

Degree has been able to successfully combat the common problem of heavy perspiration during stressful situations. This product adjusts its antiperspirant action to provide greater protection when needed, preventing embarrassing stains on clothing.

CERTIFIED STAINMASTER CARPET

Du Pont recognized a consumer demand for increased stain resistance in their carpets. The company responded with Certified Stainmaster Carpet, a specially constructed carpet with stain-resistant fibers.

Du Pont's high-impact advertisements are an excellent illustration of a market problem and Du Pont's solution. For instance, you're having a catered dinner party while your adorable son is making a mess on the carpet. But no worry, it's a Stainmaster Carpet. Those stains will come right out.

FORT LINCOLN MERCURY—NAVIGATOR

A luxury sports utility vehicle. The first American car maker to sell an upscale SUV at below-import prices. Yuppies began to show up in the "older" folks Lincoln showrooms to buy the vehicle. A huge success.

Who ends up with the bulk of the revenues and profits? Not the company that enters the market as number four with one more me-tooer. Even from a pricing standpoint, the company that provides the innovation to the consumer is the company that can command an impressive gross margin—at least until the competition follows. Innovators, not imitators, are the companies that, over time, end up with the higher returns and, ultimately, lower risk. Risk is substantially lowered, regardless of the category, competitive environment, company strengths, or investment level, if the product really solves a problem that current offerings inadequately address. It's as simple as that.

Types of Screens

U.S. corporations need to shift their thinking and risk posture. They must be willing to stand up to shareholders and say, "Earning will be down this year because we are investing in the future." While few CEOs would have the guts to make such a statement, innovation cannot occur until that mentality is instilled into the minds of corporate managers.

To set up the discussion of screening criteria, Exhibits 6.3 and 6.4 present the screening criteria for a food company and for an industrial/commercial manufacturer. While the depth and breadth of screens differ—the screens have been tailored to the specific company's needs—and have been in place for more than five years, both companies are churning out successful new products.

Different types of screens can be used to evaluate and prioritize new product opportunities. Screens can be applied to entire categories or individual new product concepts. Types of screens include:

- ✧ Strategic-role screens
- ✧ New product type screens
- ✧ Financial-risk screens

One problem that often arises in setting screening criteria for new products is establishing criteria that are too rigid and cumbersome. Again, if screens are used as clubs to eliminate

EXHIBIT 6.3 Screening Criteria for a Food Company

STRATEGIC ROLES

Improving Existing Business

- A way to increase presence and penetration in convenience stores
- A way to increase penetration and strengths in snack category
- A way to improve branded gross margins beyond 35 percent
- A means of reacting to competitive new product offerings to protect existing shares of shelf space

Diversifying Business

- A way to enter new, higher-margin breakfast foods and nutritional, health-oriented food categories
- A way to move into other refrigerated and frozen areas that offer higher margins and draw upon current process technology and manufacturing expertise and imagery transference.
- A means to further utilize equipment, plant, investment
- A means to position the company as innovative (offering more new-to-the-company and –category products and fewer extension new products)

FINANCIAL SCREENS/LINE EXTENSIONS

	Screen
Sales dollar volume by year 3	$1,000,000
Cumulative dollar volume, first three years	$2,500,000
Gross margin guideline	32%
New product profit contributions	10%
Breakeven on development and launch costs	1 to 2 years

new concepts, risk is reduced to zero, but so is growth from future new products. The use of screening criteria must be kept in perspective. Screens would not be needed if risk weren't a factor, and yet it is important to try to balance this risk factor so that screens are an asset, not a hindrance—so that they assist managers, not hinder them unduly.

The screening criteria in Exhibit 6.4 show how a consumer packaged goods company first established a set of common screens that all new concepts had to satisfy, and then applied various role-specific screens, depending upon the type of business requirement that the new product concept would be potentially addressing.

EXHIBIT 6.4 Screening Criteria for an Industrial Commercial Manufacturer

These initial screening criteria are common to all growth opportunities and match the company's overall corporate goals.

COMMON SCREENING CRITERIA
Strategic
- New products and services must fall under the category of "information processing and office supplies."
- Initially, new products must be sold through existing distribution channels.
- High-technology-based new products will be allowed into the core business only if they remain cost competitive or offer improvements in quality over old products.
- New products must have limited product liability.
- New products must capitalize on internal strengths.
- Patented technology
- Service/distribution
- Commodity-type products
- High volume
- Currently loyal customers
- Professional and broad-coverage sales force
- New products in the core business have priority.

Financial
- New products must generate a positive cash flow within two to three years of launch.
- New products must have a 15 to 20 percent ROI after three to five years.
- The difference between gross profit and total incremental costs to carry a product line as a percent of sales should be 8 to 10 percent of the pretax profit.
- New product expenditures over $500,000 must be reviewed by the officers.

TYPE OF PRODUCT
Role
- Cash generator/diversification.

Strategic Screens
- Must fit into information-processing or office-automation supplies category.
- Must have similar selling characteristics as core business.
- Must be able to be sold to existing customer base.
- Must be adaptable to direct sales and distributors, and current customer base must be using it in large quantities.

- Must have long-term, secure relationship with suppliers.
- Must be a high-quality product.

Financial Screens
- Minium return on investment is 10 to 15 percent by year 2.
- Revenue threshold is $500,000 by years 2 and 3.
- Pretax margins of 8 and 10 percent by year 2.
- A minimum of 7 to 8 inventory turns annually.

INTERNALLY DEVELOPED NEW PRODUCTS

Role
- Long-term growth/diversification and protection of core business.

Strategic Screens
- Must be in the information-processing or office automation products category.
- Must provide adequate diversification to core business.
- Must have long-term growth potential.
- Must be as good as competitive products.
- Must fit with current customer base.
- Must be at least as profitable as core business (profit margins).
- Must be compatible with current sales force.

Financial Screens
- Minimum return on investment of 15 to 20 percent.
- Timing to break even in 2 to 4 years.
- Pretax margins should be a minimum of 10 to 12 percent by year 3.

ACQUISITIONS

Role
- Protection and growth of core business/long-term growth/diversification.

Screens
- Acquisitions must offer increased capacity, cost savings, and/or resources that complement current operations; i.e., customer base, sales force, technology.
- Acquisitions should be in distant geographic areas such as the East or West Coast.
- Acquisitions may require higher returns (ROI) of 25 to 30 percent, as opposed to core business, which might require an ROI of 15 to 20 percent.
- Acquisitions in new business must provide adequate diversification from core business.

EXHIBIT 6.5 Strategic Roles Screening Criteria

REQUISITE   OPPORTUNISTIC

• Secure dominant product share
• Penetrate Canada
• Enter mass-merchandiser channel
• Increase shelf-space exposure
• Utilize waste byproducts
• Convert nonusers of existing product

• Manufacture and market differentiated consumer product
• Utilize off-season capacity; offset business cyclicality
• Exploit existing technology in a new way
• Produce price-competitive industrial product
• Establish foothold in new geographic market
• Utilize existing production capabilities

COMMON CRITERIA FOR ALL ROLES

• Category growth at least comparable to inflation rate
• Fragmented competitive market with new national consumer packaged goods manufacturers
• Utilizes similar distribution/transportation network
• No high-technology component

• Premium-priced, high-margin, value-added differentiated consumer product
• Distributed primarily through grocery trade
• Raw material related to product
• Production process similar to product
• New Product—shelf life four to six months
• Minimal coverage of competitive product by existing broker force
• Gross margins must exceed 35 to 40 percent

• Regionally oriented business
• Product with differentiated value-added or cost-competitive potential
• Gross margins must exceed 40 to 45 percent

Strategic Role Screens

Strategic-role screens can be applied to categories *and* to specific new product concepts.

They are predominantly nonfinancial criteria that pinpoint competitive, market, or other key business requirements new products will have to fulfill. Exhibit 6.5 illustrates a consumer-packaged-goods company with four strategic roles driving its new products program. In turn, each strategic role has differentiated screening criteria based upon varying levels of perceived risk by each role.

Once categories have been selected, strategic roles are often

EXHIBIT 6.6 Consumer Packaged Goods Company

New Product Strategic Roles	Product Screening Criteria	
	Sales Threshold	ROI
Enter the Emerging Under-21 Market Segment	$20 Million	20%
Establish Foothold in a New Geographic Market	$10 Million	25%
Increase Share of Shelf Space at Retail	$5 Million	15%
Utilize Off-season and Excess Capacity	$2 Million	12%

the first set of criteria to use against any new idea that emerges within selected categories. They are the bridge to a company's corporate objectives because they describe what a company expects from any new product. Apart from the desire to increase revenue and profit growth, strategic roles help to explain: Why are we focusing attention on new product development and what do we expect to gain from our efforts?

Strategic roles must be agreed upon by all levels of management. Otherwise, new product development is chaotic. Disagreements over directional interpretations and priorities will lead to mass chaos and poor communication, with each manager pursuing his or her own strategic goals. The company ends up spending dollars and committing people to projects that are "out of sync" with its best new product interests.

The following examples of strategic-role screens are from two companies: an equipment manufacturer, and a consumer-packaged-goods company. These strategic roles define which business requirements new products are expected to satisfy. Any new product concept must satisfy one or more of these strategic roles.

Equipment Manufacturer

✦ Defend core business against competitive inroads and ensure company survival.

✦ Expand target customer base to secure new users

✦ Strengthen company's position in supplier attractiveness to current target customers.

✦ Decrease cyclicality of earnings.

✦ Fill obsolescence gap in product line.

✦ Utilize excess plant capacity.

✦ Offer way to move company into other high-
growth, high-margin product categories.

This company selected strategic roles that were largely aimed
at strengthening the company's existing operations. Only the
last role is expansive, reflecting the company's concern with
using new products to first bolster its business before branch-
ing out into new areas.

Consumer Packaged Goods Company

Requisite roles—improving existing business

✦ A way to increase presence and penetration in
the dairy case.

✦ A way to increase penetration and strength in
the cereal category.

✦ A way to improve branded-product margins.

✦ A means of reacting to competitive new product
offerings to protect existing share of shelf space.

Expansive roles—diversifying the business

✦ A way to enter new, higher-margin cereal, cereal-
related, and dairy categories.

✦ A way to move the company into refrigerated
and frozen areas that offer higher margins than
the dry shelf.

❖ A means to further utilize the breading- and bev-
erage-packaging-equipment investment.

❖ A means to position the company as an innovative entity that offers more new-to-the-world and
new-to-the-company products and fewer line
extensions.

This company chose to separate its strategic roles into requisite
and expansive roles. For this company, new products were
needed to defend the existing business as well as to diversify
into new businesses. Clearly, this company saw new products
as tools to build market share.

Financial screens can also be established for strategic roles.
As the investment required and the probability of failure increase for a product, the performance expectations should go
up. A useful approach in assessing risk relates the required investment level to the probability of failure for each new product. The calibration of risk varies by strategic role. For
example, a new product that utilizes excess capacity, fits the
current distribution, and requires minimal investment can be
assessed as low risk. (See Exhibit 6.7.) Establishing a foothold
in a new country may also require little investment. However,
the probability of failure is higher, and therefore the new product would be assessed as a moderately high risk.

Each role may have a return estimate tied to it—based on different perceived levels of risk:

❖ Low risk (15 percent ROI required). New products that will utilize excess capacity.

❖ Moderate risk (20 percent ROI required). New
products that will serve to combat a new, competitive entrant.

❖ Highest risk (25 percent ROI required). New
products that will enable the company to establish a foothold in a new country.

This company has clearly decided that as its financial strategic
roles become more risky, it will, in turn, require higher ROI
performance from those new products selected to fulfill each

EXHIBIT 6.7 Relationship Among Strategic Role, Investment, and Risk

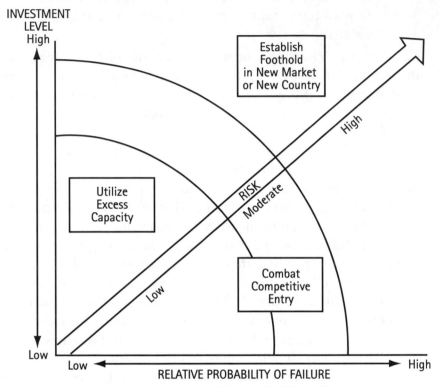

Squares represent strategic roles the product is trying to fill.
Risk is a function of the size of the required investment and the probability
of failure for the new product. Risk increases along the diagonal as investment
and probability of failure increase.

role. The screens become stiffer and more difficult to pass as risk increases.

To summarize, strategic-role screens are broad statements that putting forth the various business conditions that new products will have to fulfill in order to pass through the screening process. They are largely nonfinancial but do include finance, market, and competitive concerns and internal requirements. They are strategic in nature because each one contains some basic element or issue of vital concern to the company.

New Product Type Screens

While each new product type has a different level of risk, the smart company will adjust the financial return expected by the product type to reflect the varying risk level. For example, the revenue and profit minimum should be substantially less for a lower-risk line extension than for a high-risk, new-to-the-world product. Here, in particular, the issue of differentiated screening criteria becomes especially relevant. The point is to establish financial screens that reflect the relative risk to the company by each new product type.

The screens for new product types illustrated below are well understood by management in this company. They have been discussed several times and agreed to by all managers involved in new product planning. Managers in this company understand why these three new product types are the only ones included in their screens, and they have agreed to work within the framework of options.

- ✧ *New-to-the-world*—Rests on the premise that consumer need is best met in a whole new way. Consumer must be able to see or understand the benefit of the product and its use.
- ✧ *New product line*—Must be perceived by consumer as outperforming competitive product. Exceptional price/value relative to need.
- ✧ *Flanker*—Expands consumer interest in existing product line.

For a company that has been extremely successful at commercializing new-to-the-company products, the relative risk of this new product type may be less than even a line extension.

The determination of risk level by new product type should be a function of three factors: (1) company past experience with a new product type; (2) internal strengths that will consistently be brought to each new product type; and (3) a balance of new product types in the planned portfolio. If a company wants to introduce only new-to-the-world products, the risk level for those new product types is substantially higher than it might be if other lower-risk new product types were also part of the new product strategy.

The following example illustrates how some companies establish qualitative *and* quantitative screens by new product type *and* strategic roles, as shown in Exhibit 6.8. In this case, while the consensus of top management in a consumer durables/ and nondurables company was that the use of new product screening criteria would help focus the new product effort and increase the chances for new product success, no distinction was made between strategic role or new product type. Five screens were established for all new concepts and categories.

- ✧ All new-to-the-world or new product lines must be technologically superior to any existing product on the market.
- ✧ All new product lines for the division must be in categories where competition is fragmented.
- ✧ Stay away from high-spend, advertising-intensive categories and competitors unless product is unique.
- ✧ Must be able to reach distribution channels economically.
- ✧ After commercialization, new product projects must be formally reviewed if they fall below $500,000 in revenues or under 20 percent profit margins.

These five screens provided just enough guidance for this company to keep a handle on its new product efforts. However, further breakdown by strategic role and new product type would have given the company more focus and direction, and made their screening process more beneficial.

Financial Risk Screens

The financial screens should be the final set of screens for a new product concept. After the business analysis has been completed, and there is a moderate degree of comfort regarding the demand and cost dimensions of the concept, a pro forma statement can be assembled. With a projected income statement in place, a new product concept can be evaluated against

EXHIBIT 6.8 Example of New Product Screening Criteria for a $300 Million Durables Company

		Qualitative Screens	Quantitative Screens (by year 3 after launch)
STRATEGIC ROLES	Preempt competition and defend share	Must generate at least a 2% market-share increase	20% ROIC
	Expand into foreign market	Affords the formation of a new consumer business	25% ROIC
	Utilize waste byproduct	Must be distributed via existing channels	12% ROIC
NEW PRODUCT TYPES	New to the world	Must utilize in-house technology patent	$5 million sales, 40% gross profit margin
	New to the company	Competition must be fragmented; no two competitors with over 70% share	$3 million sales, 35% gross profit margin
	Line extensions	Must be perceived by consumers as better than competitors' offerings	$.5 million sales, 25% gross profit margin

the new product financial screens. Exhibits 6.8 and 6.9 show the different kinds of financial benchmarks that can be used and the great range in numerical sizes and expectations. Obviously, risk profiles vary dramatically among companies, a fact reflected by the degree of risk companies are willing to take with financial screens.

The lack of specific screening criteria may have contributed in the past to a diffusion of new product efforts. Management has made major strides in developing more precise criteria by new product type. (See Exhibit 6.9.)

After business analysis and product costing, new product concepts must pass the quantitative screens before prototype development and plant testing. (See Exhibit 6.10.)

As Exhibits 6.9 and 6.10 demonstrate, financial screens are

EXHIBIT 6.9 Financial Screens by New Product Type

Product Type	Revenue Size ($ Million)	By Year	Minimum Operating Profit Margins	By Year	Payback Year
New to the world	$5 to $25	3	20%*	5	3
New to the company	$5	3	20%*	3	2
Flanker (protect business)	$1	2	5%	1	2
Line extention (adds to)	$.5	2	At least equal to existing margin	1	2
Repositioning	At least equal to existing product	1	At least equal to existing product	1	1
Cost reduction	At least equal to existing product	1	At least equal to existing product	1	1

*And/or a minimum ROCE of 30%.

most often tied to new product type or strategic role. In this way, financial screens can be differentiated according to varying levels of risk. A higher financial hurdle will be set for the roles or new product types that will require longer development and investment time and costs and less clearly defined consumer demand. Launching line extensions that increase plant capacity should involve relatively low hurdle rates. Thus implicit in the screens is a calibration for the varying degrees of risk.

The reason it is important to set differentiated screens rather than a single hurdle rate is because missed opportunities usually occur when a company sets up only one standard performance benchmark. A consumer packaged goods company has consistently stated that it will launch only new products that represent a $25 million new product opportunity within three years. They have just as consistently not launched any new products during the past four years. Are there no profitable $18 million new products that would make sense for this company to launch? The point is that when one single standard is set for all new products, many potentially successful new products are neglected and ignored. Yet developing some sort of financial screens is essential to ensure that the financial expectations surrounding new products are viable.

EXHIBIT 6.10 Quantitative Screens

Minimums	New to the Company	Line Extensions	Flankers	Resale
Revenue volume by year 2	$500,000	$250,000	$100,000 (By end of year 1)	$500,000
Cumulative revenue volume by year 3	$1,500,000	$750,000	$350,000	$1,500,000
Gross profit	24%	21%	20%	20%
Pretax margin	6.0%	5.5%	5.0%	5.0%
Breakeven—payback on development and launch costs	3 years	2 years	1 year	3 years
ROIC	5-year payback	3-year payback	3-year payback	5-year payback

---

Challenging the Screening Criteria

The following questions serve as a checklist that should be used once screens have been developed. Challenging the integrity and comfort level of the screens will reinforce a company's adherence to them in the future.

- ✧ Are the new-to-the-world criteria too aggressive?
- ✧ Are there past successful new products that would have been screened out under the present criteria?
- ✧ Will the use of screening criteria be perceived within the division as a mechanism that cuts off the "creative juices" or helps direct them?
- ✧ What will be the effect of the criteria upon new product projects currently on the books?
- ✧ Are corporate financial objectives consistent with the new product screening criteria?
- ✧ How will the screening criteria be effectively adhered to?
- ✧ Have we left any noticeable gaps in the criteria, and if *so, why?*

Developing Screens: Find Out First

A final note on screening criteria: It is important to find out what management perceives as the key criteria for judging new product opportunities. You may be surprised at the results. Usually, managers have several screens in mind that they will elaborate on when asked. Whether the criteria have ever been communicated to other managers is another issue. But talk with at least three or four managers to see if any patterns emerge. This information can also provide a starting point for listing and formalizing a set of screens that management can ultimately agree on. You will probably want to talk with managers in all functions related to new product development, including research and development, corporate/divisional business planning, finance, sales and marketing, and human-resource management. Begin by making a checklist of questions to guide each interview. Afterwards, compile a draft of potential screens and the pros and cons for each screen, and circulate them to all interviewees. After comments have been collected and you have had a chance to synthesize and develop a final group of screens, you should find greater acceptance of them, because people have had the opportunity to take part in developing them from the outset. Don't forget senior-management involvement. You may decide to involve senior management in this process for political reasons, even when senior managers have little direct involvement. This will give you some "political protection" down the road.

In Summary

Screening criteria serve as the game rules for the new product development process. They should be used as tools—not clubs—to assist in the management of a diversified portfolio of different types of new products. Risk can be managed— screening criteria will provide the guideposts.

CHAPTER 7

Igniting the Development Process

The role of technology as the "fuel cell" for innovation is instrumental and fundamental. This isn't a quantitative issue. . . . It's about the ability to create new applications, products, and possibilities . . . that didn't previously exist and raise the competitive ante in ways that other improvements, though important, can't match. . . . There are many examples of how a new technology has broken through previous constraints to satisfy latent customer needs.

Kuczmarski, Middlebrooks, and Swaddling, *Innovating the Corporation* (Lincolnwood, IL: NTC Business Books, 2001), p. 203.

A new product development process can be compared to a road map. It provides the direction and the routes to take to get to the final destination—commercialized new products. With enough resources backing it, just about any process will work. However, given limited human and financial resources, the process needs to be tailored to a company's specific needs. Often, companies never take the time to establish the direction-setting needed to optimize the allocation of resources. Rather, they believe that a cauldron of hot new product ideas is the right place to begin. Generate some "big" ideas and we'll be successful. Wrong! Unfortunately, for those types of companies the boiling pot continues to be stirred, but few successful new products are ever cooked up. One reason most companies tend to experience a 50 to 70 percent failure rate in commercialized new products is insufficient direction-setting up front.

The Need for Discipline

Managing new products successfully requires a commonly applied, disciplined process that is consistently used and understood by all managers. Companies use a variety of approaches to develop new products. While no single process is suited for all companies, there are common elements among effective processes that serve as the foundation for constructing a company-specific new product process.

This first stage of the management process tells managers where the company wants to head with new products and the role they should play in meeting the company's objectives. Driven by longer-term objectives and business strategy, the direction-setting stage has been discussed in the previous chapters:

- ✧ New Product Diagnostic Audit—Evaluates the past new product performance, strengths and weaknesses, and pinpoints internal impediments.
- ✧ New Product Strategy—Defines the growth gap for new products, goals, strategic roles that new products will satisfy, and screening criteria to be applied to new product concepts.

These gearing-up steps may require anywhere from three to six months to complete. Again, a company cannot afford to give short shrift to this gearing-up stage of the process. Once these steps are finalized and top management has given its blessing to the direction, new product strategy, and category priorities, the direction-setting part of the process should now guide development activities for at least the next twelve to eighteen months. Often it is most productive to leave a new product strategy un-

EXHIBIT 7.1 New Product Development Process

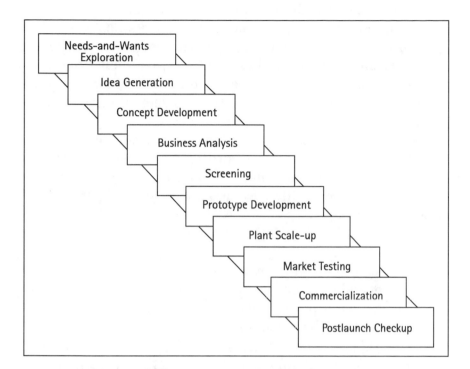

touched for first two years to give the new product team time to work against the same objectives. However, there is nothing wrong in updating the strategy on an annual basis. Just don't totally redirect the new product strategy each year. If you do that, the only new product will be a planning document.

A balance is needed. Once a solid directional plan is prepared, adopted, and approved, then choose the development process and stick to it. Of course, frequent referral to the new product strategy, screens, and so on is paramount in order to keep the development activities focused. Once the direction-setting stage is completed, management will have a road map that guides development activities. This stage enables new product participants to know the agreed-upon game plan and the routes to take to get there. The blueprint and new product strategy will be used throughout the development process.

A client who was the new product development manager for a $300 million food company wanted to get going with idea generation, because he had some aggressive new product objectives assigned to him. He saw no need to prepare a new product strategy. He firmly believed that a strategy was the planning department's job. Top management quickly informed him that the value of the blueprint was to solicit from other functional managers their perceptions of the role for new products. This step really helped to build ownership among managers in the development process.

With the new product direction set, the ten-step development process offers a logical approach for taking a selected list of potentially attractive categories and generating ideas from them that will eventually become new products. Following are the ten steps:

1. *Needs-and-wants exploration.* Examine external market and competitive trends, ascertain potential needs and wants of each customer segment, and identify problems that customers cite.
2. *Idea generation.* Through a variety of problem-solving and creative approaches, generate new ideas that fit the identified categories.
3. *Concept development.* Take ideas that pass initial screens and develop a user-friendly description of the product.
4. *Business analysis.* For each concept, formulate a market and competitive assessment that leads to a pro forma for two to three years.
5. *Screening.* Keeping in mind the financial forecasts developed in the business analysis, pass the remaining concepts through all performance criteria.
6. *Prototype development.* Complete development of product and run product-performance tests.
7. *Market testing.* Determine consumer purchase intent; test the product in either a simulated market or actual market roll-out.

8. *Plant scale-up and manufacturing testing.* Determine rollout equipment needs and manufacture product in large enough quantities to identify bugs and problems; run product-performance tests.

9. *Commercialization.* Introduce the product to the trade and consumers.

10. *Postlaunch checkup.* Monitor performance of the new product six and twelve months after launch relative to original forecasts; after one year, performance is monitored annually.

Here is a brief description of each step:

1. *Identify potential wants and needs of each customer segment.* Before idea generation begins, exploratory market and customer research is an essential component of the new product development process. This vital stage provides the foundation and platform for effective idea generation. It offers tangible needs, wants, gripes, complaints, and problems that customers have about a certain activity, function, or products/service performance.

For example, when Kuczmarski & Associates was helping Rubbermaid's Office Products Division develop new product concepts, the consultants undertook exploratory upfront research and talked with administrators, purchasing agents, salespersons and executives about their office-related problems and needs. Many managers told us that they were using their automobiles as extensions of their offices. With the advent of the cellular phone, the car had turned into a mobile mini-office. But the problem was, "My passenger seat ends up cluttered with papers, files, pens, and tapes. It's a mess." This problem fueled the generation of a new idea that Rubbermaid ended up commercializing.

The product was the Rubbermaid Auto-Office™, which was positioned as a car-seat desk system to "make every mile count with this mobile office organizer." It provided hanging folders and file storage, a writing surface, and compartments for storage. The point is that this innovative new product solved a customer problem: how to keep the passenger seat of a car organized.

EXHIBIT 7.2 Examples of New Products that Solved Customer Problems

THERMOSCAN—THE INSTANT-READ THERMOMETER

When my doctor used this product to take my temperature, I immediately sensed a new product success in the making. It offers a great advantage—instant thermometer readings from the ear. In fact, infrared tympanic thermometry, in effect, records the infrared heat generated by the eardrum and displays a person's temperature in less than two seconds.

Imagine how much easier it is to take a child's temperature. There are multiple problems that this product is solving including the need to get a thermometer reading fast and the difficulty of taking a child's temperature. Then there is the hygienic advantage of disposable probe covers that virtually eliminate any cross-contamination safety concerns. And temperature readings are more accurate.

POWER POINTER AND KODAK EKTALASER POCKET POINTER

The Power Pointer is a pocket-sized laser pointer that projects a small ruby red spotlight. Designed for visually directing attention during lectures and presentations, it can be used to pinpoint areas on charts, graphs, and the like, while the presenter stands some distance from the screen.

Kodak's Ektalaser even has a blink mode in which the red spot flashes. (Of course, flashing red spots may also be used in waking up your audience after you've been speaking for a while.)

The *problem* this product solves is the inability of a presenter to reach the screen with an ordinary hand-held pointer. More uniqueness in a product usually brings a higher price value.

CANON PLAIN-PAPER FAX MACHINE

Remember the thermal-paper fax machines? They were the rage until 1989. But that year, 50,000 plain-paper fax machines were sold. Acceptance grew swiftly with over 150,000 plain-paper machines sold or leased by 1990. There are a number of methods of producing faxed images on plain paper including laser, ink-jet and thermal transfer.

Canon's Laser Class Fax uses a laser process to print images on plain paper. What are the key benefits of this product from a problem-solving standpoint? There are several including no smudges, no ink all over your hands, no curling as with thermal fax paper, and less fading. Most critical is that with the plain-paper fax there's no need to make a copy of the fax as was usually the case with thermal fax paper.

EXHIBIT 7.3 Ways to Identify Potential New Product Ideas That a Company Can Consider

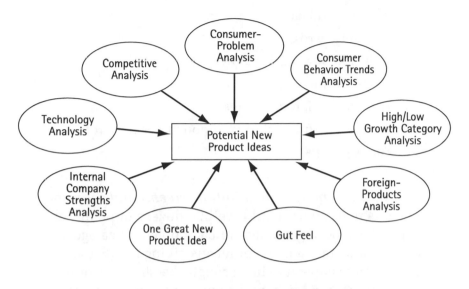

Three other examples of new product launches that stemmed from identifying problems, needs, or wants early on are described in Exhibit 7.2. Exploratory research prior to idea generation provides a basis for creative solutions for specific problems, needs, or wants.

2. *Generating ideas in selected categories.* Now there is a road map in place to begin the creative, brainstorming, and association-making process of developing new ideas. As depicted in Exhibit 7.3, companies can utilize a wide variety of approaches to generating new product ideas. New ideas hardly ever seem to be lacking in companies. There are, however, a number of tools and approaches that can be used to solicit emerging ideas.

 ✧ One-to-one interviews or group sessions with
  • Employees across functional areas
  • Management
  • Suppliers

- Customers
- Competitors
- Sales representatives

✧ Patent searches

✧ Warranty cards

✧ Questionnaire and surveys

✧ Trade shows

✧ Trips to foreign countries

✧ Purchased and customized consumer research

✧ Focus groups

3. *Develop concepts, conduct initial screens, and set priorities.* At this point, there could well be dozens of potential ideas that have been generated in each potential category. Turning an idea into a concept means giving the idea form, substance, and shape: making a rough sketch, envisioning the type of package, the price, and so on. The concept must describe the real, functional, or perceived benefits of the new product concept. The task is to apply screening criteria *loosely* to each concept. *Loosely* is the appropriate word. All the in-depth business analysis should be completed later in the process. That then becomes the data base to screen out or in specific new product concepts.

The process of developing new products is iterative. Each step builds on previous steps. Therefore, some initial screening takes place here to determine which concepts warrant business analysis. Granted, a dose of judgment is required at this stage in setting concept priorities, but keep in mind that a number of screens—those aligned by strategic role or new product type—have already been developed to assist in this process. Implicit in being able to screen concepts is the need to have some "homework" completed on each concept to develop a rationale for attractiveness. Thus, a minimal amount of analysis, including an examination of competition, relative market shares, key success factors, growth of the category, and degree of capital intensity should have been preliminarily examined by now for any concepts under consideration.

4. Conduct business analysis of selected concepts. Business analysis of a new product concept requires examining the dynamics of the category and the competition, cost positions, consumer buying patterns, and fit with internal strengths in order to develop financial projections. Specific components of business analysis should include the following:

- Market trends and growth potential
- Competition
- Distribution structure
- Environmental considerations
- Complementary product performance
- Barriers and costs to enter and serve the market
- Success and risk factors
- Product unit costs
- Product-performance ratings by consumers
- Consumer segments and concept reactions
- Fit with company strengths
- Financial projections—income statement and capital requirements.

5. Screen concepts to determine prototype candidates. Once the business analysis has been completed for a concept, it should then pass through the quantitative financial screens that were established in the new product strategy. This is often a good go/no go point to get approval from management to proceed further to the prototype development stage.

6. Develop prototype. By this stage in the process a mockup, a sample, or some other type of prototype often has already been developed by this stage in the process. But now is the time to design a product that is final to the extent that cost of materials and manufacturing can be accurately figured. Moreover, manufacturing must by now be actively involved with the research lab or engineering staff. Much time is wasted when manufacturing is handed a product that just won't work outside the lab.

The objective at this stage of a new product's development is to get one or more protoypes that are in final form for consumer testing, can be costed, and can be made. New product managers must remain involved—they cannot just turn the project over to the technicians. A product champion must nurture the product concept through this stage, especially since coordination among several functional departments is required.

7. *Run product-performance, customer-acceptance, and market tests.* Companies often forget this stage. Excitement, anticipation, competitive threats, and management emotion begin to creep in. A product has now been developed, it passes the screens, management "knows" that it is going to be a winner, so why perform more tests?

The answer is to make sure it really is a winner and to make the product even better. The objective of a test market is to determine whether a new product will fly and what changes need to be made prior to launch. However, the main advantage is to provide real-life direction on how to improve the positioning, packaging, pricing, advertising, and shelf placement. In this way, a company reduces the risk of failure during commercialization. While test markets do take time and money, the questions a company has to ask if avoiding this stage are: Can we afford not to test this product? What are the potential upsides and downsides if we don't?

8. *Initiate plant scale-up.* At this point, the decision to launch or not must be made. Additional equipment may need to be purchased, factory lines shifted, new tooling added. The product needs to be tested in the plant in large enough quantities to ensure product quality prior to launch.

9. *Develop launch plans and commercialize new product.* Timing, coordinated and carefully planned execution, and communication are the cornerstones of a successful launch. Once the test results have proven adequate and the decision is to go forward, the sales force must be brought up to speed and properly motivated to garner their commitment behind the product. Often companies neglect this important step. The sales force must be sold just as the consumer must be persuaded to buy.

Moreover, the execution of the launch must be properly

timed, adequately supported, and closely monitored to make adjustments to the initial program. Identification of the target customer, product positioning, and competitive advantage must be factored into the development of the rollout plan. The underlying cause behind many product failures is poor execution during this phase of the process. A new product may still be further refined during the first six to nine months in the marketplace.

10. *Monitor performance regularly against the original plan.* This step, often overlooked by companies, can provide significant leverage in the development of successful new products. Management frequently "revises" forecasts once the new product has been in the marketplace for six months. The original financial estimates are forgotten, and by year 2 no one in the organization has any recollection of what they were, never mind measuring performance against them.

Encouraging Disciplined Creativity

The "creative," right-brain manager may dream up ideas all day rather than follow through with those ideas and create a tangible product. After shooting down a formal approach to new product development, that manager might shout, "You're stifling creativity and innovation with all these processes, screening criteria, approval points, and business analyses."

The reality is that a number of different approaches can work. The important thing is that a company choose one process, agree to the steps and approval points, and stick with it. Ideas must be carried through to commercialization or killed along the way based on a sound rationale—not emotions. Irrationality commonly develops unless a company brings managers along to reach a common understanding of the process to be used. Top management runs the risk of being brainwashed into believing that constant change in the process and a "mucking-around" approach to new products yields the creativity needed to come up with the big winners. Not true.

Successful new products absolutely do result from heavy

doses of creativity, but creativity occurs more reliably when there are stimuli, such as information, inputs, feedback, analysis, custom problems and association-making. Each of these stimuli can nurture and spark idea generation. Most companies create practical ideas more frequently when there is a formalized process in place. Disciplined creativity breeds successful idea generation.

Corporations have limited funds, resources, and time. Yet the creative dreamers believe they should be given free reign to magically produce new ideas. Most companies are not short on new ideas, but they are short on ways to assess, screen, prioritize, and execute those new ideas.

Some new product people have somehow deluded management into believing that new product management is not a multidisciplinary process but rather a creative free-for-all. This thinking must stop if a successful, well-managed new product program is desired. First, find a sound business leader—a seasoned manager with strong leadership qualities. Put him or her in charge of your new products development program and make sure that top management becomes the coaches and champions for the process.

The Need for Consistency

One distinctive characteristic of successful companies is that they keep the same process in place for a period of years. You can't have a bunch of new product managers all going in different directions, using various approaches to generate the next great invention of the decade. Uniformity provides a team experience that focuses on results rather than on the means of getting there. Disciplined creativity is the best approach.

Successful companies have a systematic, disciplined and orderly process with sequential steps that guide the development of an idea into a commercialized new product. It is a step-by-step process, and at the same time, it is an iterative process. That is, the outputs of each step can be looped back to the previous step in the process. While each step of the process is distinct, each overlaps and is tightly linked to the other steps surrounding it. For instance, after you have finished concept development, you may have moved to business analysis; but if in conducting this step, two additional ideas are generated that look promising, these ideas need to be recycled back through the concept-development stage at a later time.

Using the same process uniformly yields the most productive results. While companies use a wide variety of processes and approaches to develop new products, the most successful companies are those that have kept the same process in place for more than five years. A new product development process provides a thinking and action framework for transforming new product objectives into commercialized new products.

Management is often enamored with changing the new product process. Many believe that if the method by which new products are being developed changes, increased creativity will result. The opposite occurs. New product managers become confused, often lost, disillusioned, and frustrated. Creativity is subdued rather than nourished. The art of managing new products is a creative and "flowing" activity in and of itself. Therefore, companies need some anchor to hold onto—structurally sound and sturdy girders that new product participants can erect around the program.

At this point, you may be asking yourself: Should a new product development process be structured, systematic, orderly, disciplined, and done by steps, or should it be adaptive, flexible, iterative, and tailored to company objectives? The correct answer is yes. All of those attributes depict a sound process. The MAP System™ itself is ordered and structured, yet at the same accommodates the uniqueness of every company.

The major benefit of having one process in place for a period of time is that it produces economies of scale. Managers involved in the process develop a comfort level after working with the process for a few years; they see how consumer problem identification works; they understand the purpose of strategic roles better. They increase their efficiency during every stage of the process. The best companies are those that are able to keep the same team of new product managers in place for a relatively long time.

That's how a company really gets leverage from its new product people. Once a new product team has generated a couple of hits, team members increase their collective and individual self-confidence. Top management is also apt to feel more confident in this group and, therefore, to be more committed to the new product effort.

Yet for some strange reason, many companies continue to perpetuate a certain attitude: New products is only an area to get your feet wet for advancement purposes in the company. You don't want to stay there long, because you need to be in an operating unit to get promoted. How short-sighted! Give me a manager any day who can generate and launch a successful new product. It takes more skill and more seasoned managerial capabilities to effectively manage a multidisciplinary team working on new products than to run a momentum-driven, well-defined existing business.

Companies need to emphasize that new product development is a promotable and career-advancing position. While the risks are higher, the benefits that accrue to successful performers should be recognized. The best people should be in new products for at least three to five years. It must not be a revolving door for less effective managers who are placed in a career holding pattern.

Solving Common Problems in the Development Process

Once a company conducts a diagnostic audit, the flaws and shortcomings in the new product development process can be more clearly seen; however, even then, it may be difficult to sell the changes that may be needed for enhancing the effectiveness of the process. To prove that your company is not the lone wolf in the wilderness—the only organization that has problems—here are some of the problems commonly found in the development process across large and small companies:

> ✧ Prototype development is well under way before in-depth market analysis has been completed and business potential determined. If the decision is not to go ahead with the product, R&D managers react negatively when they consider

all the time they spent that now goes down the drain. A frequent complaint expressed by R&D people is, Why didn't they estimate the size of the market and discover that the competitive barriers were too great before telling us to spend three months developing a prototype? Why wasn't market analysis done prior to giving us a mandate to develop this concept?

✧ New product priorities often shift, and not all new product participants are aware of the change or understand the rationale behind the new priorities.

✧ Subjective, emotional, and political judgments influence critical-path decisions too heavily.

✧ Screening criteria are overlooked and circumvented.

✧ Process steps need to be simplified and streamlined. One company we worked with had a process that consisted of forty-three development steps—much too cumbersome and counterproductive.

✧ The process lacks flexibility and adaptability. A process that is rigid and regimented will curtail individual thinking, product championship, and motivation.

✧ Lack of clear approvals and go/no go decision points that provide closure and specificity, since screening criteria are loose.

✧ There are variations in interpretation of the process and meaning of the steps across different functional areas. Marketing's interpretation of the business analysis is different from that of research and development or finance.

✧ Not enough focus and attention placed on test marketing—often perceived as unnecessary. "This product is so great, let's just roll it out nationally, before our competitor discovers the idea."

❖ Too many approval points and checkpoints in the process. Top management becomes an obstacle to getting anything done—approval is always needed before moving to the next step.

❖ R&D and marketing not working jointly or closely together from idea generation to test market.

❖ Sales and manufacturing input not secured or used until the plant scaleup and test-market stage commence.

❖ Infrequent and ineffective communication mechanisms, thereby leaving new product participants working in the dark.

This litany of common development-process problems supports the need for a commonly understood and adhered-to process. Here is one area where discipline and structure are required. You cannot have new product managers running around a company developing new products according to their own approach. There is plenty of room for creativity—in idea generation and concept development—but not in the process used for developing new products. Establish an effective process and then leave it alone. It is fine to maneuver around it at times, but leave the goal posts in place so that the new product players know on which end of the field they should be playing.

The following example, which summarizes the obstacles to the development process identified in one consumer-durables company, may help you spot problems in your own company.

The company had been failing at new products for at least five years. While several factors—not just the process—were contributing to poor performance, several fairly common process shortfalls that were contributing to the overall problem did surface. The major issue was that the company still did not have a systematic process or method in place for managing and controlling new product development. It just more or less "happened" in the lab, the focus group, the conference room, and the manufacturing plant. While there was one new product director and a new product team that met monthly, the focus was on status updating and the progress made since the last meeting instead of content discussions regarding next steps. Among the shortfalls that management identified in its process were the following:

- ✧ The lack of strategic guidelines to focus new product and acquisition efforts. There were no "guideposts" that managers could use, nor was there a road map to follow.
- ✧ Lack of clear accountability and responsibility for new product development.
- ✧ Lack of overall direction and coordination of the steps in the process.
- ✧ Idea and concept generation was hit-or-miss rather than deliberately focused on a category, strategic role, growth area, or anything.
- ✧ Very limited business analysis prior to prototype development. The tendency was to "let the lab people get started on this thing. It always takes them so long." Of course it took the lab people a long time. They were being inundated with superfluous new product concepts.
- ✧ Weak communication, coordination, and sporadic involvement among functional areas in shepherding a new product from concept to commercialization.
- ✧ Lack of communication with, and especially feedback from, "new product participants," including customers, sales, manufacturing, marketing, packaging, and brokers.
- ✧ Lack of lead time for development and distribution of sell-in materials to the sales force for a new product launch.
- ✧ Realistic timetables and deadlines not set or not adhered to during the steps along the process.
- ✧ Limited pilot testing and market testing prior to commercialization.

✧ Limited product performance testing, for example, quality control, shelf-life stability, packaging, or consumer acceptance prior to roll-out.

✧ Cost analysis conducted too late in the process. Volume and profit projections were not tied into concept development.

✧ No written or formalized screening criteria for setting priorities, evaluating concepts, or measuring performance. Many low-volume products and discontinuations resulted.

✧ Insufficient project accounting or monitoring system. No idea of how much development costs were running.

✧ Inconsistent tracking of post commercialization performance of new products launched. No understanding of why new products succeeded or failed.

✧ Lack of decision-making forum at top management level to steer strategic direction of new products.

This company addressed their new product problems with its board of directors and was soon on the search for a full-time new product manager. Once he was hired, the company underwent many changes to its process. Three years later, new product results were impressive: twenty new products launched, $38 million in incremental revenues from new products, $2.5 million in incremental profits.

One of the best ways to determine why the current new product process is not working as planned is to distribute a written survey to top management that solicits their own perspectives on the way the current process works. The sometimes telling results of such a survey allow top management to see clearly the discrepancies among the ranks. There has to be agreement among the top players on some of the basic elements of the process. That is one of the major causes underlying a failing new product process: everyone in the company is coming from a different direction with different internal rules and policies.

Thus identification of process problems is a key step in improving the effectiveness of new product management. Once the problem areas are agreed upon, solutions can be created that will then become integrated into the new product process.

Key to Process Effectiveness

Any successful new product development process is structured and systematic. Participants must be able to envision the progress of an idea through to market launch and to plan the route to be taken. Flexibility should be allowed in order to accommodate external market changes, such as competitive moves, entry into a foreign market, or a new patent discovery.

Moreover, the process should have distinctive steps through which concepts pass. New product people need to know what stage of development a new concept is in at any given time. Management should also require separate steps to ensure that clear approval points can be established, for example, after business analysis, prototype development, and test market.

Most important, top management and new product team members must apply the process uniformly. They must establish a clear understanding of how the process should work in order to enhance day-to-day new product management. Furthermore, new product participants should feel they have some room to move within the process. Unless they have some freedom, creativity and championship will not emerge. However, the freedom provided must have some boundaries—it must work in a given framework.

Used consistently and interpreted similarly by senior managers as well as by functional and new product managers, the process must include frequent communication. Constant communication, feedback, and dialogue with new product team members and top management is needed to keep all informed and abreast of progress made and obstacles observed. A mix of formal and informal communication vehicles is usually most effective, including such things as monthly meetings and stopping by an office to see how things are going.

Clear approval points should be set up in the process to clarify the go/no go decision points for any new product concept. Moreover, the process should spell out *who* makes these decisions and how they make them effectively. Tied to the approval points is the need for the process to be definitive in describing accountabilities for new product activities during each step of the process. Who is responsible for tasks and coordination efforts must be outlined at the outset.

The consumer-durables company discussed earlier, after identifying the shortfalls in its new product development process, made several changes in the way it went about structuring innovation. Some of the steps that resulted in a successful track record were to:

- ✧ Decide, agree upon, and implement a commonly understood step-by-step development process that includes clear-cut approval points.
- ✧ Ensure adherence to the process steps in a consistent and timely fashion.
- ✧ Begin prototype development after completing the market assessment and business analysis of the concepts.
- ✧ Increase input from potential customers during the concept, prototype, and test-marketing stages.
- ✧ Adhere more closely to screening criteria and terminate unattractive product concepts early in the process.
- ✧ Conduct rigorous market research tied to competitive, business, and market-opportunity analysis.
- ✧ Tighten the integration and communication link between sales, marketing, R&D, and manufacturing.
- ✧ Conduct more frequent field testing prior to commercialization.
- ✧ Define coordination responsibilities and accountabilities.

Having checkpoints throughout the process is a good way to keep people on track and enables top management to have access to the process.

Typically one of the key missing ingredients in a company's process is adequate homework: compiling external market and customer information that will serve as the backbone for decision making, assumptions development, and screening. If managers select new concepts on gut feel, the risk jumps exponentially. That is not to say that intuition is not an important factor because it is. But concepts cannot be passed through screens unless the competition, market, consumer, and costs are examined. The people managing the process need to get their hands dirty in the category and business analysis. They need to think, look, and listen as they continue to shape and mold a new product.

After the approval for commercialization of a new product, there should be someone continuously monitoring the new product's performance. This will allow managers to make course corrections, product or marketing changes, and adjustments to the product. If the product encounters severe problems early on, a monitoring system will detect them, thereby limiting potential losses. Changes in the product or even termination could result from monitoring. Monitoring performance of new products relative to original objectives will result in better forecasting because of the lessons learned and the new product track record that is established.

Bolstering forecasting skills through better business analysis is a commonly perceived need. Of course, if there were any sure-fire way to project accurately the future performance of a new product, we could have eliminated the risk element of the process a long time ago. However, the statistical models that clutter the new product testing and forecasting fields are not the solution. Statistical models cannot guarantee to do much better in forecasting than can someone who objectively develops assumptions and examines various external and internal factors.

While there are no money-back guarantees in forecasting, looking back at the performance of new products and comparing actual to original project usually provides a way to measure the variance that occurs. After some practice, a new product manager should be able to discern some patterns. For example, most forecasts for certain types of products were over, under, or within a close range of target projections.

Screening new product concepts more rigorously, conducting more competitive analysis earlier in the process, and market testing products prior to commercialization represent the most neglected parts of the process.

Choosing Categories

An effective approach to idea generation is to focus on three or four categories that represent attractive opportunity areas for a company. In this way, the team focuses the new product concepts into predetermined high-potential areas. The concepts themselves still need to be passed through additional screens, but this will produce a far more efficient result.

In the following example, I discuss a consumer-durables company that had established a blueprint for its new product program. With a $5 million annual new product budget, management wanted to be sure that some "big hits" would occur. Their new product strategic roles focused on identifying attractive categories that would offer unique products that consumers would use for household tasks or time-consuming projects.

The thrust of the company's new product strategy was to launch new products that would create a totally new business for the company. Line extensions, product improvements, and repositionings had characterized the new product program in the past. Now management wanted an aggressive effort placed on new-to-the-company or -world products, not just modifications to existing products.

As a result, the following guidelines were established to focus all category identification and new product idea generation.

> ✧ Identify, evaluate, select, and commercialize new
>   business opportunities for branded non-durable
>   products as well as small, hand-held durable
>   goods.

✧ Primary focus—identify opportunities that form the nucleus of new consumer businesses.

✧ Secondary focus—develop new product additions that renew, defend, or expand current product lines.

✧ Enter markets or market niches where there is an opportunity to become the dominant or leading player in the line of products.

The identification of potential categories for new product opportunities should *precede* the generation of ideas and concepts for individual new products.

Market information is critical before developing new product ideas and concepts. You should ask yourself the following questions for each category under consideration.

✧ What are the current entries and who are the key competitors in the category?

✧ Where are the gaps in the category and how do you fill them?

✧ Who is the consumer?

✧ What differentiates currently successful products from those that are less than successful?

✧ What benefit are consumers seeking in the category?

✧ What new product trends can you see in the category?

There is more involved in the process of category identification than just listing a few attractive categories that appear to offer opportunity. To do it right, it may take a new product group three months to give adequate time to this important step. The time investment in category screening will pay off once idea generation begins.

The most essential part of category identification is thinking carefully through the development of business visions. Take, for example, the business vision of air-purifying equipment. A company is looking to expand into the retail home market and decides that its technology can be used to make air purifiers for the home. However, after looking into that category, the company sees that sales in air purifiers have declined during the past five years, consumers are unhappy with the effectiveness of given purifiers, and foreign competitors have entered the field. So management decides not to enter this category.

Unfortunately, the business vision had not been carefully expanded or thought out. If the opportunity had been defined differently, that is, the business vision broadened, the company might have found itself developing successful new products in a growing category. Air deodorizers and air fresheners had been growing at more than 15 percent per year in dollars during the previous five years. This is the category that would have been identified if the business vision had been expanded. A different business vision could have provided a strong opportunity for this company. It already had a technology that could be applied to small table-top models that not only absorbed odors but also released a fragrance to cover any remaining telltale odors in the air. The business vision might better have focused on products that could provide consumers a way to control or absorb odors from the air. From this starting point there is a good chance that some preliminary category analysis would have uncovered the attractiveness of the deodorant-and-freshener category.

Let's examine the steps that can be helpful in category identification before idea generation for specific new products begins.

> ✧ Develop a "gut-feel" list of initially attractive categories with a selected group of internal managers—a top-of-mind list of categories without any analysis. Any company should be able to generate at least ten or twenty different categories that might be feasible for new products.
>
> ✧ Next, further expand the list of potentially attractive categories, perhaps to twenty or thirty, through individual interviews and group meetings with

- R&D
- Top management
- Sales
- Marketing and business unit managers

◇ Judgmentally prune back the list of categories to fifteen or twenty that fit the new product strategic charter of the company, which has already been defined.

◇ Conduct preliminary analysis on the first-cut categories to establish a data base and rationale to determine potential attractiveness.

◇ Develop qualitative category screening criteria to be applied to each of the fifteen to twenty categories.

◇ Select five or six categories that fit the charter and category screens and have an internal champion or sponsor.

◇ Review the target categories with top management to solicit its insights, comments, and consensus.

◇ Begin idea generation and concept development within the identified categories.

Categories that survive the screening stage are ready for idea and concept generation. Companies can take several approaches to idea generation. The key component to idea generating is making associations. One thought leads to another and sparks a new thought from someone else. Most important, idea generation is a *group* rather than an individual endeavor. Sitting in a dark room by yourself, contemplating new product ideas, will usually yield few results. However, the power of group dynamics turns on creativity.

There are several ways to prepare a group for idea generation. A group needs to be warmed up before it can generate new ideas. Beyond the need for strategic roles and the like to provide some order and structure to idea generation, group members need grist for their minds. Opinions and information from a wide variety of sources can be instrumental in sparking ideas. This body of information should be distributed at least one week before the idea group meets to allow time for some association making. Some background sources include interviews with suppliers, brokers, distributors, customers, noncustomers, focus groups with potential customers or distributors, and a company suggestion box. Other sources include questionnaires/surveys, purchased market research, and visits to other parts of the country or the world.

Often informal one-to-one interviews or group sessions stimulate new product ideas and offer additional background for an idea-generating session. Special insights may be contributed by:

♦ Sales representatives

♦ Employees—marketing, engineering, manufacturing, service

♦ Management

♦ Suppliers

♦ Customers

♦ Department meetings

While this list is far from exhaustive, it suggests that there are many underutilized and untapped resources that companies can draw upon to sharpen creativity.

After categories have been selected, the development steps are used to generate ideas, develop concepts, analyze the business opportunity, screen, develop prototypes, market-test, and commercialize the new product.

In Summary

Grounding the development steps in a direction-setting framework can enhance the management of the new product development process. Establishing a systematic, structured process will enable new product team members to follow an ordered approach, increasing efficiency of the effort. While creativity is an essential component of any new product process, a certain degree of discipline is healthy. Moreover, it is imperative that a company does not keep changing its development process. Consistency in using one process is more effective than trying to redo the process frequently. While a variety of approaches work, companies that follow and adhere to the steps established will be more successful in commercializing new products.

PART IV

The People

This section covers the most important component of the MAP System™: People. Managing and motivating people in ways that make them feel valued, accountable, and rewarded is the key that unlocks the door to innovation superiority. The best companies truly understand that strategies and processes are important for accelerating innovation, but that their success depends on the extent to which the people in their organization believe that they can take risks, make mistakes, pursue true breakthrough innovations, and be rewarded for failure—yes, even failure.

The truth and value of the old saying that whatever gets measured, counted, and rewarded is almost always what managers and employees will pay attention to is reflected in the last three chapters of the book. Thus, beginning with the belief that the need to develop metrics for measuring and evaluating the outputs and performance of innovation investments is tantamount to planning for future successes, Chapter 8 outlines the key measurements that every manager can use and every team member can work toward. Chapter 9 identifies the best ways to organize a new products effort. Chapter 10 shows how to motivate and reward top performers, and Chapter 11 gives the key insights into creating the kind of culture that brings it all together.

8

Measuring Return on Innovation

> **W**hat is the most important thing to remember in establishing innovation measurements? Demonstrate the value. . . . show how measuring innovation leads to better results . . . and how the information can be used to drive improvement.
>
> Kuczmarski, Middlebrooks, and Swaddling, *Innovating the Corporation* (Lincolnwood, IL: NTC Business Books, 2001), p. 243.

People need and want metrics and measurement tools that help define where they should go based on where they've been. You can only manage what you can measure. And measuring risk and return is what this chapter is all about.

Innovation Spirit in the 21st Century

As we approach the 21st century, executives will undergo a radical change in the way they run and grow a business. They'll use innovation as a core business strategy and as a way to gain competitive advantage. They'll create an innovation mindset that permeates their organization. They'll take risks.

Creating "newness"—whether in the form of new products, or new services, or new marketing programs, or new channels —is becoming the first thing senior managers are turning to for earnings growth—not the last. Most future managers will stop cost-cutting and depleting valuable human resources. Instead, they'll find new and innovative ways of utilizing their people to create and discover new growth opportunities. It will be an exciting period in the economic progression of our country. People will be taking risks and having fun growing businesses.

In fact, a continued surge in earnings growth will stem from a renewed commitment to creativity and innovation by "winning" U.S. companies. We'll be able to feel and sense a "spirit of innovation" in many companies. People will believe in the power of innovation. Economic growth in this country will continue to escalate.

Consequently, companies will want to monitor and keep track of their investments in and returns from innovation. They'll need to know how much bang they are getting for their innovation bucks. Measuring the effectiveness and efficiency of innovation dollars and people resources will become critical.

Of course, once the right measures are in place, rewards and compensation need to be aligned to those measures. Managers and employees need to be compensated for the risks that are inherent in developing new products, new services and new breakthroughs. New compensation approaches must be put in place to reward actual market place performance and results.

But the spirit of innovation needs to find a way to soar in large Fortune 500 corporations where it is currently dampened. The innovative spirit is found in smaller, entrepreneurial companies. The internet has spawned more risk-taking environments than have ever been seen before.

The fact is that employees are jumping from large companies (5000+ employees) to smaller ones (100 employees or fewer). From 1990 to 1994, 7.7 million employees were added to under 100 employee companies while 3.8 million left large companies.

Creating corporate cultures that accept risk-taking as a core tenet of the workplace will provide the platform for innovation success.

If new product innovation is so vitally important to the growth and prosperity of companies, why have senior managers and executives been so reluctant to encourage innovation and risk-taking in their organizations? The short answer is: the lack of a set of standard metrics to measure and manage the risk associated with new product innovation. This chapter is devoted to showing how new product innovation can be measured and, therefore, managed.

Measuring and Managing the #1 Barrier—Risk

Executives from more than 200 U.S. companies have participated in the "Winning New Products and Service Practices Survey," which was conducted in concert with Kuczmarski & Associates and Northwestern University's Kellogg Graduate School of Management. The survey identified the top five barriers to innovation in their business organizations:

Top Barriers to Innovation Success

✧ Predominance of a risk-averse culture.

✧ Lack of metrics relating to return on innovation investment.

✧ Lack of a new product strategy. They felt that they managed a product list instead of a cohesive strategy.

✧ Insufficient human resources.

✧ Poor communication between levels of management and across functions, which interfered with setting clear expectations.

Note that the first and second barriers are the hinge on which all the others turn. The inability to measure risk and the associated return on investment is what justifies risk-averse management. A standard of measurement—New Product Innovation Metrics—is key to breaking down all other barriers because it provides the data needed to help make better decisions. Metrics provide the information needed to shape a new product strategy and to track performance against that strategy. In turn, management can communicate their expectations to the company's new product teams and the entire organization. Clearer expectations and tools with which to measure performance loosen everyone's grip on risk aversion because they understand the boundaries within which they are operating. The remainder of this chapter will discuss the key performance and program metrics used to measure an organization's new product innovation efforts.

Measuring Newness

Most companies don't have any idea how much money they invest on innovation each year. They just don't keep score. Accounting systems and budgeting approaches will need to dramatically change in order to systematically measure returns on innovation investments.

Managers must be able to draw the connection between innovative effort and their results. Innovation results in one superordinate outcome—newness, whether in the form of new markets, products and services, channels, business units, segments, etc. History has proven that it is through the "newness engine" that organizations, if not entire nations, have risen above their peers to positions of strength and continuing prosperity. Those who have failed to innovate have been left behind. The British were able to build a global empire through their innovativeness by building stronger and faster fleets. The same analogy holds true in any form of competition, whether it be on the playing field or in the marketplace. Quite simply, those that innovate best, win!

Newness can be used to fuel growth and stimulate demand. The labor forces of most major U.S. businesses have now shrunk to a size where additional cost cuts in the future, like cutting off one of a horse's four legs, will not make them more able to win a race in the long run. Instead, those organizations which will succeed in the next 10 years will be those who can, through newness, introduce new benefits to the market or improve upon the robustness of those it is already delivering. Business practice has proven that the most effective manner for stimulating market demand is meeting unsolved problems with new approaches and solutions, not solely providing old solutions in a more cost effective manner.

Similarly, business leadership today must recognize the *strategic* power of innovation and the potential role for accelerating future growth. For too long innovation has been overlooked as a downright effective way to grow earnings and increase company value.

Consequently, companies should look to innovation as the major source for building competitive advantage. The watchword for the new millennium should be competitive innovation, that is, a strategic approach for preempting, protecting against, or jumping ahead of competition. By developing products and services with totally new benefits, often delivered in new ways to customers, organizations will be able to increase their customer's satisfaction and shield their business from the onslaught of competition.

Here's how it works as a core strategy. You use innovation to enhance the margin structure of your business. Adding topline revenues is certainly valuable, but new products, new services, and new marketing programs must enhance the perceived benefit of your offerings in the mind of your consumers. As the perceived value-benefit increases, the price-value also increases, and margins go up. This, of course, is the goal of innovation; however, it doesn't always play out this way.

Importantly, the time horizon for innovation as a core competitive strategy needs to be viewed over a two- three-year time period. One of the major causes of low returns from innovation is due to rushing new products and services out the door too quickly. Getting more new product failures to market faster should not be the goal. Consequently, measurements and innovation metrics can be used annually to see "how we're doing."

Ultimately, a company's innovation capability will produce greater financial performance and higher market values which, in turn, creates an increased sense of shareholder and employee satisfaction. Look at any industry and you can witness how innovation effects market leaders relative to their peers—even those considered the most mature.

Shaving: Gillette

Gillette is a perfect example of how innovation efforts increase overall corporate performance. In terms of innovation commitment, Gillete has spent close to 2.5% of their annual sales figure on research and development over the past decade. Their management encourages and rewards risk-taking and, like mutual fund or stock portfolio managers, accepts failure as an inherent and unavoidable byproduct of taking such risks. Gillette avoids "gimmicky" line extensions in favor of "true" innovations and significant products improvements. To preempt competition, it creates internal product competition wherein new product teams are encouraged to self-cannibalize existing Gillette products. And in terms of pure innovation output, $.40 of every sales dollar which it earns is from products launched during the past five years.

What have been the results of such efforts? Looking at the time period from 1991 to 1995 (because Gillette purchased Duracel in 1996), revenues rose by almost 50%, operating income doubled, and stock price increased 3-fold. Not too shabby for a century-old company.

Investment Management: Charles Schwab

When it was founded in the early 1970s, Charles Schwab needed an innovative approach to even enter the brokerage market. Schwab took a common and established product (securities) and found an uncommon way of getting them to consumers (remote service and technology) and an innovative position (discount brokerage). But, it has been Schwab's innovative efforts beyond market entry which propelled his firm to an annual compounded growth rate over the past two decades of over 20%. Schwab's recipe for success:—significant investment in new products, new markets and new, internally-efficient processes coupled with an almost religious belief in getting close to the customer to uncover unmet needs.

The results have been a virtually unbroken string of continuous industry innovations, from computer technology which offers immediate order confirmation, to 24-hour-a-day, seven-day-a-week service, to electronic trading from one's own personal computer. Probably the best example stems from Schwab's identification of the customer's need for one-stop shopping of diversified mutual funds. Schwab responded with the introduction of One Source, allowing for a single point of purchase for more than 350 no-load mutual funds in 50 different fund families, bundled into one single account with one monthly statement. Schwab's mutual-fund assets have since grown from $6 billion in 1991 to more than $60 billion in 1996, making it the third-largest mutual-fund distributor in the United States. Over the five-year period dating from 1991 to 1996, revenues more than tripled ($570M–$1.85B), operating income more than quadrupled ($50M–$230M), and stock price and earning per share increased 4-fold ($10–$40 and $.29 to $1.30 respectively).

Key Principles for Measuring Innovation

While the argument for innovation is convincing, innovation by definition is difficult to measure by traditional means. Management's reluctance to embrace innovation is found not in its ability to understand it, but rather its ability to measure it. They feel, and maybe rightly so, that if it cannot be measured and made tangible, it cannot be controlled and therefore cannot be managed. Yet, most every manager will agree to the power of innovation. Realizing this, the only alternative left is to attempt to measure the returns on innovation.

The Strength is in the Simplicity

The fact is, the metrics used to evaluate new product and service innovation are easy to understand and easy to compute. These straightforward metrics have proven to be useful for clients in very different industries. And, they are meaningful for everyone in the organization—from the Board of Directors to new products team members. These metrics derive their strength from their simplicity.

Standardize, Standardize, Standardize— And Commit!

We emphasize the value of standardizing one set of metrics. Standardization allows for comparison of metrics over time, across divisions, and even across an industry. Furthermore, standardized metrics provide a common language for management at all levels in discussing new products and service innovation.

Systematize Data Collection

A word of warning before we go on: It is almost certain that by deciding to use these metrics, you will be required to delve into the dark corners of your firm to find data. Take heart, though. Once you identify the sources of data, establishing an on-going system to track and maintain the data can make this measurement process manageable in the future.

The Step-by-Step Guide to Measuring Return on Innovation

1. Appoint a team of people to establish the Return on Innovation measurement program. This team will be responsible for deciding which measures to use, establishing a systematic data collection process, and calculating the first set of metrics. We recommend including at least one finance person and one marketing person familiar with the new product development process. If you have a heavy volume of new products to track and measure, it may also be wise to bring in a data base programmer to make this process even easier over time. While it is possible to keep these metrics in simple form, a data base will make collection and calculation easier to do.

2. Starting with the list of innovation metrics, select those that are best for your firm. Not all the metrics may be relevant to your firm. For example, a telecommunications client decided that the "R&D Innovation Emphasis" metric would not be meaningful due to the role of an outside R&D entity, Bell Labs, in developing new platforms.

3. Construct an ROI data collection process. This process should include the standard rules and procedures for measuring ROI as well as the roles and responsibilities of each of the ROI team members. Remember that in order for ROI to work, the process must be consistent from product to product.

4. Establish a standard time period, whether one year, three years or five years, over which to calculate the metrics. It may be difficult to go backwards for the first year or two, but we advise taking a three- to five- year outlook for most industries. Three years is appropriate for industries where the product life cycle is short, such as technology and entertainment industries, while five years is better for durable goods and services industries.

5. Establish a list of new products. Define each product by product type: (a) new-to-world, (b) new to company, (c) line extensions, (d) new positionings.

6. Record the date the concept passes each step of the formal product development process. Ideally, your firm has a formal new product development process that identifies key steps and approval points, so that you can identify exactly when a product begins each step. For example, you might have three key dates on your list: (a) concept approval, (b) market test start, (c) product launch date. Plus, a fourth date is necessary for recording the "kill date" when the development on a new product stops, either to be put in the "freezer" for future use or into the cemetery of dead ideas or failed products.

7. Collect the data. Exhibits 8.1 and 8.2 outline the data needed for calculating these metrics. For the revenue and profit numbers, a general rule is to stick to the accounting numbers your finance department uses so that the numbers are readily accepted by management. There are a few exceptions to that rule that will require special tracking.

One area that may require special tracking is the development costs. You will need the cooperation of the human resouces department to track payroll and expenses that are related to each new product. You may also have to establish a time and

EXHIBIT 8.1 New Product Metrics

Performance Metrics	*Program Metrics*
• Return on Innovation Investment (R2I)	• R&D Innovation Emphasis Ratio
• Cumulative Profits and Revenues	• Innovation Portfolio Mix
• Growth Impact	• Process Pipeline Flow
• Success or Hit Rate (3 yr.)	• Innovation Revenues per Employee
• Survival Rate (3 yr.)	• Speed to Market

expense reporting system for the team that works on new products, especially if the team is staffed by special assignment rather than by full-time positions.

Usually it is best not to include corporate overhead costs as part of the expenses, since those costs can cloud real product contribution. And certain costs may need to be allocated on a pro rata share, such as advertising costs that cover a broad range of products.

New Product Metrics: Setting the Standards

The first step in managing new product innovation is to develop common, consistent standards for measuring all aspects of the Innovation Investment across as many dimensions and business units as possible. Two basic kinds of metrics—Performance Metrics (those that measure growth) and Program Metrics (those that measure and reflect program management and control) cover the key dimensions of Innovation: the Plan, the Process, and the People. (See Exhibit 8.1.)

There are no hard-and-fast prescriptions for which measures are the best to use. Ideal measures will tie to a firm's new product strategy. Metrics *should* be tailored to each firm. They should also be organic so that new measures can be added over time.

New Product Performance Metrics

Innovation Performance Metrics look at both the short- and long-term performance and impact of the new product development program on the firm, thereby minimizing knee-jerk reactions to short-term issues. They include Return on Innovation Investment (R2I), Cumulative New Product Revenue and Cumulative New Product Profit, Growth Impact, New Product Success Rate ("Hit Rate"), and New Product Survival Rate.

Return on Innovation (R2I)

This is the number that attracts the most attention, especially from CEOs and the investment community, because it is the most useful in demonstrating performance. Like ROI—return on investment—R2I also shows return on investment, but only from new product *innovation* investments, not all investments. It looks at the firm's total profits from new products (cumulative new profits generated from new products launched) divided by its total expenditures for new products. This long-term ratio shows the firm's total return from new products over a three- to five-year period. This number has two uses:

1. Descriptive: to demonstrate the overall effective contribution of new products.
2. Predictive: to forecast or set goals for the organization.

Total expenditures should contain all components of all costs for:

- ✧ Research, including market research, customer research, and concept testing.
- ✧ Development, including product definition, product design, prototype development, and actual product development.
- ✧ Incremental production, including tooling, facilities, and employees.
- ✧ Initial commercialization and pre-launch, including market testing, communications development and media costs.

EXHIBIT 8.2 Return on Innovation Investment

R2I is driven by all the other metrics, since all have an impact on the bottom line. Just as with traditional measurements, managers focus on this number alone and ignore the other measures at their peril.

$$\frac{\Sigma \text{ Cumulative Net Profits Generated from New Products Launched}}{\left(\begin{array}{c} \text{Research} \\ \text{Costs} \end{array} + \begin{array}{c} \text{Developemnt} \\ \text{Costs} \end{array} + \begin{array}{c} \text{Incremental} \\ \text{Production} \\ \text{Investments} \end{array} + \begin{array}{c} \text{Intitial} \\ \text{Commercialization} \\ \text{Prelaunch Costs} \end{array} \right)}$$

Cumulative New Product Revenue and Cumulative New Product Profit

These numbers, which show new revenue produced versus spending, are especially valuable for forecasting and planning, in particular because they show what is working. When developmental spending is placed side by side with gross revenue and gross profit, managers often gain new insights into their new products programs. Maybe the gross revenue is lower than expected. This might mean looking at the original strategy or elements of its assumptions or execution. Maybe net profit is lower than anticipated, which could mean that an adjustment in operations or production is needed. Or, better, gross profits are higher than expected, which could mean that top management has a template for other new product development opportunities.

Growth Impact

There are only two ways to get new business—make or buy. As has been described in Chapter 1, acquisitions can be just as risky as new product innovations—even more so. This number shows the concrete contributions new product innovation is making to organization growth. Growth impact is derived by determining the percentage of the total company revenue growth for a period (typically three to five years) represented by cumulative three- to five-year new product revenue, expressed as:

Growth Impact= $\dfrac{\textit{Cumulative 3- to 5- year revenues from new products}}{\text{Total company revenue (for same period)}}$

This metric can serve as an eye-opener when board members and Wall Street realize the percent of revenue growth over three to five years in relation to total revenue growth.

New Product Success Rate ("Hit Rate")

Management should be sure to look at the success rate of the overall new product portfolio so as to not overreact to the inevitable failures. One measurement method is to divide the number of new products exceeding the 3- to 5-year original revenue forecast by the total number of new products commercialized over the same period. Simply stated:

Hit Rate= $\dfrac{\text{Number of new products exceeding original 3- to 5-year revenue forecasts}}{\text{Total number of commercialized new products}}$

Of course, success rates vary with industries and companies. As a benchmark, companies should not expect more than a 65 percent success rate for all new products launched. An extreme variation from this percentage probably means one of two things: (1) products are not being categorized properly; (2) the company isn't taking sufficient risk in its new product programs.

New Product Survival Rate

Firms must look at more than just the number of products launched in one year. They need to determine which of those survived a couple of years and are longer-term successes. This lends clues to whether the products met customer needs, met product quality targets, and lasted long enough to recover costs and earn a profit. The firm's new product survival rate is the

number of launched products still on the market divided by
the total number of products launched over a specified time
period. Or:

$$\frac{\text{Number of commercialized new products still on the market}}{\text{Total number of commercialized new products}}$$

Program Metrics

Innovation Program Metrics are used to understand operational concerns reflected by the Innovation Performance Metrics. Program Metrics include R&D Innovation Emphasis Ratio,
Innovation Portfolio Mix, Process Pipeline Flow, Innovation
Revenues per Employee, and Speed to Market.

R&D Innovation Emphasis Ratio

If firms expect big results from new products coming out of
their R&D programs, they need to monitor the share of resources—capital and personnel—spent on new product development versus maintenance and cost reduction programs. This
can be measured by taking the total of R&D expenditures allocated solely to new product development over a 3- to 5-year
period, divided by the total R&D expenditures over the same
time frame.

Innovation Portfolio Mix

This measurement shows the percentage of new products
commercialized by number and by revenue and is a key in
the development of the Performance Metrics categories. Of
course, "new" is a relative term. Categorizing by the following is helpful:

✧ New-to-world
✧ New-to-company
✧ Line extensions
✧ Improvements

The first two categories—"new-to-world" and "new-to-company"—are where the new product gold is. As I mentioned previously, line extensions and incremental improvements have their place in new product programs and strategies. However, these are most likely used as defensive tactics. For example, line extensions in packaged goods are used as often to deprive competitors of shelf space as to provide customers with a truly "new" benefit.

The spread of new products will tend to vary by industry, but there should be a fair representation of new-to-world and new-to-company products. These are every company's building blocks.

Process Pipeline Flow

When it comes to new products, too much can be as bad as too little. A company can be strangled if too many new products are launched and they aren't timed properly. For most companies, this means keeping a reasonably steady flow of products that the company's sales and marketing groups can sell effectively and that customers can assimilate productively. Measuring the number of products at various stages of development enables executives to control the process. Basically, a thorough schedule that identifies all critical-path functions and operations is a good place to start.

Innovation Revenue per Employee

This figure, the result of dividing the total annual revenue from commercialized new products by the total number of employees devoted to innovation initiatives, can be used as a basis for developing new product incentive programs.

Speed to Market

For some industries, this number is absolutely critical. But even for companies not in high-pressure, time-sensitive industries, time is still money. The sooner you have your new product on the market, the longer you are able to profit financially and strategically from the advantage it provides. Unfortunately, some companies focus on this characteristic to the exclusion of others, in particular, market knowledge. Technology has reached a point where virtually anything is possible. The question is less about how fast should we make it. But: what should we make?

Conclusion: The sequence is still Ready, Aim, Fire. Know your market first.

What New Product Metrics Do

Since innovation by its very definition is intangible and not easily measured at the front end (especially at the outset of a program), the logical place to begin is at the end—at the Return on Innovation Investment (R2I). Measuring R2I makes the intangible tangible, thus providing managers, employees and the investment community with valuable information that can be used in a number of ways. Here are some examples:

- ✧ **Benchmarking.** R2I measurement establishes a method for tracking performance against your company, your industry, your competition and the rest of the business community.

- ✧ **Diagnosing.** Measuring R2I helps identify and evaluate those processes and strategies that can help an organization meet its growth and strategic goals.

- ✧ **Allocating resources.** In conjunction with the benchmarking and diagnosis described above, measuring R2I enables management to determine how R&D levels, team resources, portfolio mix and other collateral should be altered to achieve company goals.

- ✧ **Compensating employees.** Measuring R2I aids in evaluating and rewarding new product teams and establishing a credible link between new product performance and corporate incentives.

✧ **Informing markets.** Measuring R2I sets a common measure for markets and outside investors to evaluate an organization's future earning potential relative to its industry peers. As a manager, this will increase the chances that your company's market value is properly determined.

✧ **Setting future goals.** Measuring R2I helps senior management set organizational direction and establish future innovation strategies.

Innovation in Action

Metrics should be applied to all three dimensions of the MAP paradigm—the plan, process, and people. To that end, you can improve your company's R2I by applying the tracking data in any (or all) of the following ways.

Plan

By strengthening the link between company strategies and innovation efforts, you can ensure that your organization is focused on the right types of new products. Moreover, you can better judge whether or not you have adequate resources to accomplish the task. An innovation plan should have three components:

1. Vision—a concise, future-oriented statement that is closely linked to your company's corporate vision and defines the boundaries and provides direction for innovation efforts. Example: "Within ten years we will be recognized as the global leader of home leisure and recreational electronic products. Our unique and totally new-to-the-world products will transform the way we—and our consumers—currently think about leisure and participate in recreation. We will leverage proprietary technology and state-of-the-art advance-

ments to create products that consumers have not yet
even dreamed of. We will make it happen."

2. Strategic roles—a guide for the types and priorities for
future new products, defining the specific functions
that new products serve in supporting the company's
growth goals. These roles may include requisite roles
—functions that new products can perform to bolster
existing business—or expansive roles, ways in which
new services can propel the company into new segments, markets or businesses. Determining the desired
mix or requisite and expansive new product activities
can help a company actively manage its new product
portfolio to achieve the desired risk/return balance.

3. Growth gap—pinpoints the quantity of new products
required and the corresponding revenues/profits from
new products expected over the next five years. By
determining this gap, a company can identify the
amount of new product activity (and the corresponding resources required) to achieve its goals.

Process

By improving the steps and sequences of new product development activities, you can provide your company with the appropriate structure and timely executive guidance to rapidly
move high-potential new products through the pipeline. R2I
data can help accomplish this mission by providing input for:

✧ A formalized new product development process
that outlines the sequence and timing of steps
that a team must perform to move projects forward. The metaphor we use most often to describe the process is a funnel. Broadest at the
top, it enables the team, and the company as a
whole, to capture the greatest number of ideas at
the earliest stages of the process. At this stage,
there are no bad ideas, though of course, some
will be untenable. That evaluation takes place
through the use of a series of criteria used to

screen out ideas that aren't so much "bad" as
simply not suited to the company.

✧ Screening criteria, which may vary by strategic
role, can objectively eliminate ideas and focus
on those with the highest potential. The criteria
should be designed so that as a product moves
through the development process, the screens
get tighter and the hurdles become more specific
so that eventually only the highest-potential new
products get through.

Equally important, this formalized process—known to everyone in the company—isn't something that happens "over
there," in some secret enclave in the company. It encourages
participation from everyone in the company and, in addition
to drawing on the broadest range of insights, it fosters buy-in
from all areas of the company. Thus, it casts the broadest net to
generate new ideas and gets the most participation possible in
evaluating those ideas in their best possible light and achieving the greatest number of successes.

People

It's no secret that the best-conceived innovation plans and most
thoroughly developed innovation processes cannot succeed
without the appropriate human resources to execute them.
Thus, the "people" components of the innovation effort must be
applied and managed correctly. Here are some suggestions:

✧ Create dedicated, diverse innovation teams—
groups of individuals acting within the charter
of the innovation plan and under the structure of
the innovation process to develop new products
and services for the organization. Effective innovation teams increase speed-to-market by bringing structure, synergy, dedication and unified
focus to what would otherwise be a haphazard
and inefficient enterprise. Strive to include participants representing a variety of functions, a

wide spectrum of company (and even industry)
tenures, and ages. Those teams which are the
most diverse—with the greatest breadth of
experiences represented—generally are the
most creative and generate the largest quantity
of new product ideas.

✧ Appoint executive champions to serve as con-
duits between the innovation teams and upper
management. This action increases speed-to-
market by eliminating unnecessary layers of
management approvals and the corresponding
delays.

✧ Develop effective innovation rewards. The rewards should be group-based and employed
using a tiered structure, taking into account any
concepts which were screened out of the product development process for whatever reason.
(This will ensure continuing innovation without
fear about compensation.) Consider also the use
of non-financial rewards, such as recognition,
encouragement and promotions, which serve to
keep team members excited, enthusiastic and
committed to their innovation work.

A recent (3/22/99) *Wall Street Journal* "The Outlook" column
by Bernard Wysocki, Jr., notes:

" . . . the U.S. labor force is growing by less than 1 percent
annually . . . By 2013 labor-force growth will be zero . . .
Every employer we know is having trouble hiring young
talent . . . We're 2 years into a 10-year trend. This shortage
is going to continue." Talent, always difficult to find, will
be even more difficult to find because it won't exist—literally. Thus, a company that creates the kind of atmosphere
and process that enables all workers—but certainly young
and talented workers—the ability to stretch their abilities
and work in a collaborative, positive environment will
move ahead of its competitors in the hunt for scarce
human resources.

Managing the Measurement of New Product Innovation

A senior management committee should be formed consisting of three to four executives to analyze, interpret, and report on the innovation metrics annually. Some action steps they may take include:

1. Appoint an Innovation measurement team, to be responsible for tasks such as deciding which measures to use, establishing a systematic data collection process, and calculating the first set of metrics. The team should include at least one person with a finance background and one person with marketing credentials who is also familiar with your company's new product development process. If you have a large quantity of new products to track and measure, you may wish to add a database programmer to the team.

2. Examine the list of Investment Performance and Investment Program Metrics and choose those that are most relevant to your organization.

3. Develop a standardized procedure for collecting innovation investment data, including roles and responsibilities for the various team members. Remember that, for Return on Innovation Investment (R2I) measurement to work, the process must be applied consistently to all new products.

4. Establish a standard time period over which to calculate the metrics. Three to five years is generally best for most industries.

5. Generate a Product Portfolio—a list of new products classified according to the following categories: (a) new-to-world, (b) new to company, (c) line extension or improvement.

6. Finally, collect the data. In general it is a good idea to use standards of measure and financial metrics that internal company groups are familiar with.

In Summary

As has been mentioned throughout this book, new product initiatives are unquestionably a company's most important endeavors. And as a recent K&A study indicated, company managements are increasingly understanding the importance of those new product initiatives: Developing new products and services was cited as one of the top three strategic initiatives of firms across a variety of industries. This dramatic turnaround since the late 1980s and early 1990s—the days of severe cost reduction programs—is partly a new realization that new product innovation is where the source of growth and prosperity is. But it is also now possible, with the range of new product innovation metric tools available, to measure new product innovation much more precisely and intelligently.

With many markets becoming more and more competitive as a result of new competitors from global or deregulated markets, firms know that those who innovate best will win in the future. And it does go back to the old saying that you cannot manage what you don't measure. Management needs to accept risk, measure performance, and embrace innovation.

CHAPTER **9**

Management—Building The Organization

T echnology can be defined as know-how, and therefore technology resides in people.

Carl E. Bochmann, Partner, Riverbend Engineering, Kellogg School of Management, Northwestern University. May 13, 1991.

I have now spent the better part of this book discussing why new product development is crucial to the future of your company and what needs to be done to be successful. The tricky part now remains: How does this get done? The answer lies in the people. This includes you, the new product team, and, really, everyone in the company. None of this book means anything if the proper organizational foundation is not in place. All you will be left with is a few good ideas, a lot of good advice, and no way to proceed into the new products promised land. Creating a supportive environment for new products is tantamount to success. In this chapter, I will discuss five managerial factors that heavily influence the ability to administer the process effectively.

✧ Organization, structure, and teams
✧ Accountability
✧ Skills mix
✧ Leadership sharing
✧ Top-management commitment

199

New product management is a complex and subtle process. In many ways, successful and unsuccessful companies often share common elements in their approach to new products. They may even use a similar step-by-step process and similar criteria to measure performance. So if it isn't the development process, what distinguishes the winners from the losers in the new product game? To find the answer, we must look at how they *implement* the process. That is often where the real difference lies. Success rests upon creating an environment that is conducive to taking risks and supportive of the individuals who take them. Senior managers, at winning new product companies, recognize that problems inherent in introducing new products can be solved only by taking an interdisciplinary team approach. Sensitivity to the organizational dynamics involved in new product development is a must. It is a delicate process requiring movement of people in a common direction. Freedom and autonomy may stimulate one type of new product manager, while deadlines and tight controls may be more effective for another. Judging what works best for each manager is the solution to leading a successful new product organization.

Creating the Right Environment: Overcoming Internal Barriers

Top management in the best of companies creates and supports a positive environment for new product development. In the less successful firms, a threatening climate is often induced by top management when it focuses on short-term results, demonstrates risk averse tendencies, and fails to communicate priorities. Senior management in successful firms generates a positive climate by assigning the best managers, supporting entrepreneurial behavior, compensating managers consistent with long-term goals, and treating the process as an investment rather than an expense. This positive climate fosters superior dedication and enthusiasm for success.

Most successful new product efforts are clearly enhanced by top management commitment. Well-defined new product roles, comprehensive measurement criteria, new product orga-

EXHIBIT 9.1 Factors Affecting the Right Environment for New Product Development

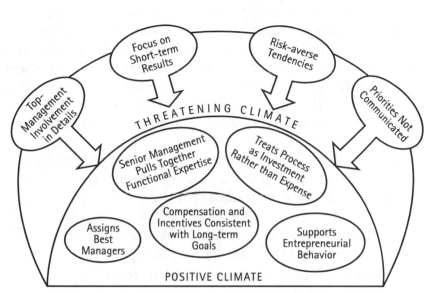

nizational incentives, and a formal yet adaptive process often demonstrate that commitment. This combination of a positive corporate environment and top management commitment provides most successful companies with a distinct competitive advantage.

The biggest obstacle to new product success today is management's emphasis on short-term profitability. By succumbing to the pressures of current business, managers restrain innovation by channeling dollars away from new products. While such an attitude may bring high profits for existing products, it paralyzes a new products program.

As management looks to new products to fuel future growth, it must overcome this short-term orientation and narrow-minded focus and commit to a sustained flow of new products to keep the pipeline full. That commitment must come in the form of long-term funding and resources necessary to realize long-term new product success.

In determining the appropriate level and extent of senior management support and involvement, companies should examine the particular types of products being developed and the management approach being used.

Top management must be willing to push responsibility down to lower-level employees by providing a high degree of autonomy. Such a venture team can then focus its efforts on doing the best possible job rather than worry about being second-guessed. Similarly, strong support from top management and extensive participation in new product decision-making can strengthen the stature of new products within a company. The strategy is ineffective unless adequate funding and personnel are available.

For example, in one company, middle managers expressed a concern that top management was not fostering a team-oriented environment. Comments included:

- ✧ The screening criteria and process steps are too systems-oriented and not people-oriented.
- ✧ Players and coaches make football teams—not referees and rule books.
- ✧ We need more emphasis on what the company can do to help people create and execute growth opportunities.
- ✧ The we-versus-they attitude needs to be addressed.
- ✧ Funding for new products is sporadic.
- ✧ Competition for internal resources by business managers curtails new product progress.
- ✧ The process is missing a market-driven thrust.

At a major chemical company, barriers that managers cited indicated that here too the right environment had not been created for managing new products. The top concerns expressed are summarized in Exhibit 9.2.

Regardless of the specific barriers in a company, the key issue is to knock them down as quickly as possible. Don't let internal barriers fester and turn into major blockades. Shrink them so that managers can at least walk over or around them.

The president of a $100 million office-products company

EXHIBIT 9.2 New Product Performance Problems Cited by Management at a Major Chemical Company

- Unclear career paths for commercial development/new product personnel
- Unclear assignment of ultimate new product responsibility
- Lack of formalized screening and measurement criteria
- Concerns regarding management's real commitment to new products
- Insufficient incentives to encourage risk taking
- Lack of a well-defined divisional *new product* strategy

---

summarized the key characteristics of his ideal new product environment, as shown in (Exhibit 9.3). Environment is an attitude and one that demands constant attention.

This all involves making changes to the company's status quo. New product managers will need to challenge the norm, and top managers will need to give them freedom to function as entrepreneurs. In turn, the entrepreneur or product champion will serve as the internal catalyst to spark innovation.

B-school mentalities withhold risktaking. Consequently, graduates who enter big corporations often feel more secure just riding with the current wave rather than trying to make their own mark in the sand. By nurturing risk taking and recognizing new product participants, companies will pave the long road towards creating the right environment.

Finding the Right People

One of the keys to developing successful new products is getting the best people to manage the process. What kind of person is the best type for new products? The ideal is a man or woman with leadership qualities and a broad and multifaceted mix of skills that provide a base for making associations and supervising numerous people and projects at once. Most important, he or she is sensitive to other people's needs and can motivate others into action by recognizing and listening to them. Communication and personal interaction is how the re-

---

EXHIBIT 9.3 Example of a Company President's Perception of an Ideal New Product Environment

- Top-level endorsement and high visibility for new products
- New products tied to long-range corporate objectives and financial plans
- An agreed-upon new product charter covering objectives, category arenas, and screening criteria
- Small-company flexibility and expediency
- Clear identification of responsibilities
- A high level of communications and interdepartmental cooperation
- Collegial, *teamwork* orientation
- Includes a portfolio of product improvements, line extensions, and new products to balance risk
- An atmosphere where failures are accepted along with the successes
- *The resources* and consistent commitment to do the job—money *and people*

---

ally good new products are developed. Can a consumer's needs be addressed if the new product people never hear what the needs are?

Too many business people seem to be so preoccupied with selling themselves upwards, downwards, and sideways that they can't seem to afford the time to listen to other people. The best new product ideas are very often found in the heads of managers within the company. However, they often remain there instead of materializing into a concept or reality, because no one is willing to listen to their ideas. What often happens is that managers are underutilized and their potential not developed. The main reason is that no one ever listens to the great ideas they may have because no one ever realizes how capable they really are. Consequently, there is a tendency to gravitate to outside, high-paid, creativity experts to generate all the answers and new ideas. Establishing a climate where *everyone* is listened to and individual ideas are respected is the foundation required to build a productive new product management program.

Cyclical and iterative thinking rather than linear and deductive thinking is the right approach. An idea does not flow in a linear progression that starts with identifying a need, eventually leading to a new product that fulfills it. Instead, it takes a core of facts, insights, observations, thoughts, and ideas from other people and blends them together through association-making process.

Part of getting and keeping a top-notch new product staff is ensuring that management is spending adequate time with the new product effort. That signals that new products are important. Top management for the most part should spend 5- to- 15 percent of its time each month on new products, and functional departments should be allocating a minimum of 20 percent of their time to new products. Any shorter time commitment stifles the momentum and diminishes the continuity of effort.

Choosing a New Product Organization Structure

Over the years, various organizational structures have been used to guide new product programs ranging from: (1) free-standing or autonomous units such as multidisciplinary teams, separate new product departments, or venture groups; to (2) functionally based units that are part of existing planning, marketing, R&D, or engineering departments.

Companies also use a variety of management styles. A progressive management style and organizational structure help to create an atmosphere conducive to the successful development and introduction of particular types of products.

From an organizational standpoint, the new product structures of companies vary widely. New product departments can either report to a division president or to a functional organization where new product activities are housed. In some cases, a separate venture group is set up to report directly to the CEO.

Perhaps one of the most interesting observations is that the way a company organizationally structures its new product activities has minimal impact on the success of a new product. Clearly other organizational dynamics must be viewed as important to the entire process, but the structure itself is not very significant. What is important is selecting *a* structure and stick-

EXHIBIT 9.4 New Product Development Organization

NEW PRODUCT DEVELOPMENT TEAM

ing to it. Constantly changing the new product organization is disruptive and counterproductive.

When dedicated resources cannot be found for a freestanding new product structure, a multidisciplinary team that draws upon different functional managers can be effective. The team approach leverages interaction of different skilled resources, facilitates decision-making, and stimulates commitment by functional departments early in the process.

However, top management must give credit to the new product team for new products launched. They also need flexibility within the guidelines of a new product strategy. Moreover, the members of the team must be provided the time to spend at least one day a week on new products. Without a minimum of 20 to 30 percent time commitment, the team concept just won't work. You cannot spend a couple of days each month on new products and expect results.

Establishing formal and informal communications will play an integral role in making the process work smoothly. The new product development team should meet weekly with the sole purpose of reviewing the status on each product, setting and changing priorities, and discussing problems. Status reports should be prepared by the new product manager to summarize the stage of development of each new product in the process. Beyond approval of the annual new product plan, the steering committee's responsibilities should include meeting quarterly to monitor progress, establish priorities, and review performance.

Two new product structures—freestanding and functional—illustrate some common structural alternatives that companies wrestle with in setting up new product organizations. The pros and cons of each are outlined in Exhibits 9.5a and b.

In short, a new product organization structure should accommodate the entire new product effort. Usually, new-to-the-world and -company products have a greater chance for success under a freestanding structure, and line extensions, cost reductions, and repositionings are better managed under a functional structure. Some type of top-management steering committee should work closely with any new product organization to set priorities and allocate resources.

A critical factor is the clear assignment of the new product management job to a single executive. This person would have total accountability and responsibility for coordinating new product activities and getting results. This strengthens the stature of new products for everyone, facilitates the execution of the new product strategy, and lessens the organizational confusion that often occurs when there are simultaneous new product efforts.

The manager's responsibility would encompass development of new product strategy and initial decisions in setting priorities. The focus of a new product manager normally is on new-to-the-world and new-to-the company products, complex line additions and product adaptations. The "new-and-improved" line extensions are usually left up to the existing business (product) manager. When the new product manager's time is spent addressing new product development activities without being encumbered by day-to-day operating pressures, the new product function has a chance of getting the time it needs.

New product managers must report to top management. No argument supports any other reporting relationship. For a very

---

EXHIBIT 9.5a Pros and Cons of a Functional Structure

PROS

- Few organizational changes required—basically status quo with additional support and analytical resources.
- Ideal if primary growth focus is on line extensions and modified products, because they are close to existing business.
- Enables product managers to use new products as a strategic tool for defending and growing businesses.

CONS

- Diversification into totally new categories and markets is unlikely—constrained by existing business bias.
- Dilutes attention paid to growth opportunities because major focus has to be on existing business.
- Without broader *diversification, growth objectives* may not be met.

---

large corporation, top management may translate to the divisional or sector president, but it does not mean that the new product manager should report to anyone lower, e.g., the VP of marketing. Otherwise, the organization is not placing a high enough importance on the new product function. If that executive cannot afford the time required to add one functional person to his or her span-of-control, it suggests that he or she just doesn't cut it.

The skills that are required of an effective new product manager rely more upon people-motivating and leadership abilities than on functional or technical expertise. The key is solid people-handling skills and experience. Yet, at the same time, the new product manager must have an appreciation for the analytical side of new product development, entrepreneurial instincts, and a sense of vision. He must also be a risk taker, a product champion, and a persuasive and motivating communicator.

Thus, the clear assignment of responsibilities provides focus for top management attention, and enhances the execution of a new product strategy.

**EXHIBIT 9.5b Pros and Cons of a Freestanding
New Product Structure**

PROS

- Autonomy and clear-cut responsibility in one manager.
- High visibility and top-management exposure.
- Fosters greater ability to control overall risk and balances new product portfolio.
  - *—New-to-the-world products*
  - *—Line extensions*
  - *—Acquisitions*
- Performance can be measured against clear-cut, isolated objectives.
- Technology resources can be focused.
- Priority setting for all new product activity can be done at one point—at the top.
- Rational resource allocation against growth modes.

CONS

- Product managers and new product director, particularly with line extensions and product modifications may duplicate market efforts.
- Product managers lose some offensive and defensive strategic control over businesses without *any* new product involvement.
- Ownership transfer issue could be negative.
- New product director will most likely not have the in-depth knowledge of existing product lines as compared to product managers.
- Clear accountability

Required Skills for the Job

One company's new product division had set rather aggressive goals. From an organizational standpoint, the division's strategy committee felt that new product responsibility should be split between the new product director and the business operating managers. The role of the business-operating manager was to be the leader in charge of managing a business category. As a result, these managers should be responsible for new products that relate to strategic requirements and roles of existing business categories. Structurally, the organization called for shared new product responsibility between business-operating managers and the new product director.

Suggestions for process improvement focused on the need for more business analysis, fewer approval points, and well-defined accountabilities. The approval process needed to be streamlined, driven heavily by business analysis, and tailored by new product type. There were too many approval points and as a result, frequent delays occurred. Management decided that four major approval points should be established:

- ✧ During new product strategy planning.
- ✧ After business analysis but prior to prototype development.
- ✧ Prior to test market.
- ✧ Prior to commercialization.

Moreover, it was felt that the process should be managed by separating day-to-day operations from new product responsibilities. People would be able to focus attention on new products rather than constantly solving other problems. Middle management recommended that full-time marketing and research-and-development resources focus on concept generation and business analysis. There would also be multidisciplinary task forces taking responsibility for execution through commercialization stages.

A new product director was hired. The job description which follows serves as a model for any new product director.

Job Description of a New Product Director

PRIMARY RESPONSIBILITY

Plan, direct, and coordinate the division's new product process through the internal development of new products and businesses, and the external development of acquisitions and joint ventures. The primary focus of the activity should concentrate on new-to-the-world products, new-to-the-company product lines, line extensions that require a technological application and new business ventures or acquisitions that would take the division into a new consumer business.

ACCOUNTABILITIES

- ✧ Assist the division president in establishing and achieving the division's new product strategic and financial goals.

- ✧ Direct the activities of the new product managers and make sure that resources are allocated appropriately to achieve growth objectives.

- ✧ Work closely with the marketing and technical directors to ensure that the new product strategy and forecasts are consistent with the division's overall strategic and operating plans.

- ✧ Develop and recommend to the management committee a new product strategy for the division. Establish demanding but achievable long-term growth and profit goals for new products.

- ✧ Monitor project progress and adherence to the goals and screening criteria.

- ✧ Supervise the development and implementation of new product and new business ventures; be heavily involved in activities and direct them closely during the first three stages in the development process—idea generation, concept development and screening, and business analysis.

- ✧ Coordinate the transfer and integration of new products and businesses into the existing business organization at the appropriate times.

Skills a New Product Director Needs

The following mandatory and desired skills are representative of those embodied in a successful new product director.

Mandatory Skills

✧ Demonstrated leadership qualities: strong people-motivating skills, solid people handling skills with experience in working effectively with various functional departments.

✧ Analysis-driven risk taker; entrepreneurial instincts and good intuition; exemplifies and encourages product champions; has vision and a positive mental mindset.

✧ Established manager with confidence and respect of peers; has personal credibility with top management—elder statesman status (not a function of age but more of business maturity and judgment); insightful understanding of, and sensitivity to, the internal culture of the division.

Desired Skills

✧ Proven track record of getting things done on time while meeting objectives.

✧ Previous line-management operating experience.

✧ Appreciates the analytical approach to new product development.

✧ Sensitivity to, and previous involvement in, the creative process.

✧ Superior selling skills—both to internal management and externalities.

✧ Strong communicator—upward, downward, and across.

✧ Well organized—strong administrative and detail skills.

✧ Good rapport with the division president and marketing and technical directors.

Skills a New Product Manager Needs

While no one may fill all these criteria, they do provide a good outline of the types of skills that are required to manage new products effectively. The following skill description typifies the strengths needed in a new product manager who would report to the director.

Mandatory Skills

✧ Tenacity to serve as a product champion or product sponsor.

✧ Creative problem solver—ability to see several alternative solutions to a problem at the same time.

✧ Strong project-management skills; can orchestrate several "balls" in the air at the same time.

✧ Exceptional follow-through and execution capabilities; solid project coordination abilities.

Desired Skills

✧ Technical and/or marketing experience; demonstrated functional expertise in one of these two areas.

✧ Strong skills base in category, market, and competitive analysis.

✧ Creative thinker, highly flexible, and adaptive.

✧ Good forecasting skills and assumptions-building experience.

✧ People motivator and coordinator.

Therefore, setting the stage for innovation calls for establishing the right organizational structure. With the right mix of people, rewarded with the right incentives, managed with the right leadership, and supported with top-management commitment most companies will be successful. Rather than going with the flow, the smart companies are trying to change their internal culture by blending structure and discipline with adaptability and flexibility.

Sharing New Product Leadership

Senior and functional management must share new product leadership. While one person needs to be held accountable for managing and coordinating the development process and also for results, responsibility for the new product discipline must be collective. Effective functional coordination and top-management involvement is needed in order to implement the development process successfully.

Learning to Be a Leader

But how is new product leadership learned and nurtured? Dr. Susan Smith Kuczmarski, who has done extensive research in leadership training, believes that leadership is a learned behavior.* According to Dr. Kuczmarski, the relevant learning process for leadership hinges on a single requirement: The learner must experience conflict. In the context of new product development, conflict is often prevalent. This may be one reason why new product experience often enhances managerial leadership skills.

However, Dr. Kuczmarski's research shows that for the learner to profit from the conflict, the experience must occur in a group that has no formal mediator. This implies that corporations with intervening or autocratic managers are not effective for teaching or learning leadership, as they are likely to influence group conflict. It is conflict that serves as the catalyst to transform a group member into a leader who takes responsibility and resolves such conflict. Thus, the process of resolving conflict in a group allows for the development of leadership skills.

Hence, to build and enhance leadership in an organization, corporate enterprises as well as entrepreneurial companies should allow some conflict in their organizational settings. This is difficult, as much of our learning experience promotes dissolution, if not resolution, of conflict. Yet to aid in develop-

---

* (The following material is reprinted with permission from Dr. Susan Smith Kuczmarski's dissertation, "Teaching Leadership," 1986.)

ing leadership in a new product organization, it is useful to nurture and perhaps even instill conflict.

Because leadership skills are acquired when individuals interact in a group, some of the parameters and variables of group dynamics are applicable to the development of those skills. It is particularly helpful to describe the group that provides the setting most conducive to learning leadership.

Three group characteristics are central to facilitating leadership development. The group must participate, be supportive, and interact informally without a mediator. Once the initial requirement for conflict is met, the extent to which the group exhibits these characteristics determines the degree to which leadership may be learned in that group.

A participating group facilitates a sense of ownership, allows members to demonstrate trust, and builds group identity. In general, participation is more easily accomplished in a relatively small group. A supportive group accommodates an identification process that serves a developmental function by enhancing the individual member's self-esteem.

The informality in the group structure allows members to experience the conflict needed for the leadership development process. Accordingly, members engage in or practice leadership behaviors to resolve their own conflicts, in particular, responsibility taking and decision making.

At some point, a group relies on each member's desire or need for a harmonious environment for its very existence. A turbulent or highly volatile organizational structure intensifies an individual's motivation to resolve the conflict. At the same time, group members act to maintain the group and build a sense of community in the face of that conflict. Group members are motivated to share leadership. They work not only to ameliorate the conflict but also to maintain and continue the group. Membership brings them a strong sense of shared values, ownership, common goals, identity, and self-esteem.

Successful group-maintenance efforts reward and reinforce members' actions directed toward perpetuating the group. These actions in turn build the group's potential for continued growth and prosperity. Activities and experiences within the confines of the group intensify the sense of community, serve a unifying function, allow a continued practice of leadership behaviors, and thereby maintain the group.

The leader should act to help his followers satisfy their wants. Additionally, the leader will facilitate the definition of any new needs felt by the individual group members as well as any new group requirements. The process is iterative and democratic. Leaders may become followers and followers become leaders.

As the process evolves, a creative leader not only appeals to the expressed interests of the followers, but also encourages a structure for constructively sharing those interests. Thus, effective leaders emerge from organizations that are closely attentive to the needs of their members.

Six Action Steps toward Shared Leadership

Here are six steps that can be used to foster leadership sharing in the new product process:

1. *A leader communicates, both emotionally and professionally, with group members.* A leader who is communicating will display and express emotions or show involvement with the feelings or emotions of others in the group. When a leader communicates excitement, recognition, integrity, and compassion, the followers perceive trust, fair play, and genuine interest in the group.

There are situations where communicating requires a display of professional expertise, i.e. knowledge, competency, discipline, and organization. Followers then perceive an understanding of goals, strategies, and relationships and the ability to handle or manage them.

2. *A leader takes responsibility for selected tasks.* Any activity in the group requires individual members to take responsibility for assigned tasks. For instance, in a planning activity, one member may be responsible for contacting members, another for providing transportation, and a third for finding and organizing the materials to be used in the planning activity.

3. *A leader nurtures and accepts criticism.* Successful infor-mal communication means learning how to attract support and receive respect from other group members.

A successful leader nurtures this activity by allowing the conflict to be processed by the members themselves. At the same time, a leader must have adequate confidence in his own leadership style and communication skills so that he can accept criticism and not be threatened by it. Leaders with self-confidence tend to trust the other members, allowing them to make decisions and take responsibility for their own actions.

4. *A leader teaches others.* Members may informally instruct others on how to handle certain parts of a job or offer assis-tance with solving a problem. In the context of a discussion group, informal teaching often occurs when one member makes a point or shares his or her personal thinking on an issue. It is a kind of teaching that generally goes unnoticed by other group members. Formal teaching takes place when members with specific competencies are given opportunities to teach others.

5. *A leader shares leadership.* Collaborating on joint enter-prises or taking collective responsibility requires working to-gether toward a common goal. This shared leadership activity demands the cooperation of each member, whether leader or follower.

A sense of collective responsibility is crucial to the group. If members do not contribute, the group does not exist. As a result, members must exhibit a strong allegiance to their group.

6. *A leader knows and uses the resources of the group.* Be-cause leaders emerge from a group, they are cognizant of group members' skills and needs. Leadership effectiveness re-quires not only knowing the specific skills and resources of each group member but calling upon the members and their skills in appropriate situations or activities.

Learning the behaviors that constitute leadership may be best accomplished through long-term involvement in a specific group. This dimension of leadership indicates that learning leadership is the result of experience—a byproduct of group interaction. The group activities, informal and formal, precipitate certain behaviors that give members the opportunity to practice playing the role of leader. The behaviors are then refined with repeated activity.

Satisfaction comes from recognizing one's own effectiveness as a leader. This sense of satisfaction is a condition that builds upon itself. Leaders feel good about their past performance and are eager to continue effective behavior. The result is self-confidence and a feeling of security.

Insecurity and low self-confidence will result in defensive leadership. Rather than focusing energy on trying to resolve conflict, a defensive leader highlights the conflict by trying to defend his or herself from existing or anticipated threats. A confident leader directs one's energies toward goals that are significant—both personally and for the good of the group.

Fostering Top Management Commitment

Consistent top management commitment, support, and involvement are essential for the success of new products. Top management must communicate the growth objectives throughout the company to ensure that there is a common understanding of the objectives, strategy, process, and organization. Assignment of the best managers to the new product positions, along with providing the required functional and analytical support, is the way to manage the growth process effectively. Top management must:

1. Ensure that a consistent commitment is made to the new product process.
2. Continue to foster an entrepreneurial environment.
3. Compensate consistent with new product objectives.
4. Be actively involved in developing the new product strategy and screening criteria.

Somehow, news about new product successes has a way of getting to top management far more quickly than news about new product failures. Accepting failure in new products should not suggest that management take a laissez-faire attitude toward the process. Effective top management does not ignore new product failures, and it makes sure that it hears about them.

Commitment to new products does not mean that only new-to-the-world products are to be pursued. Indeed, the new products garnering the highest return are those that are new to the company or the world. In fact, in examining the new product performance of seventy-five companies in the Fortune 500, we found that new-to-the-company and new-to-the-world products represented 25 percent of the products launched but accounted for over 55 percent of the companies' most successful new products.

However, some very successful new products that generate an extremely attractive return originated—sometimes literally—from the waste piles in manufacturing plants. For example, in visiting manufacturing plants at the Dole Company, a manager saw piles of pineapple sludge ready to be dumped. He applied this internal "strength" and the obvious market strength of Dole's pineapple leadership role and came up with the idea of Dole Fruit 'n Juice Bars—the category leader in frozen-juice novelties. In a similar vein, Anheuser-Busch developed a cheese-flavoring product that originated from beer spillage. The yeast contained in the beer caused a great enzyme catalyst that produced a more robust cheese flavor.

This is not to suggest that America's most innovative new products come from by-products and waste heaps. It does suggest that new products may be easy to find. The key is creating an environment where managers feel they should be linking pieces of information together to form an idea or concept that will eventually become a new product. Managers need time to make associations, need exposure to a variety of resources, and need patience to nurture a concept through the internal barriers of a company. Top executives often lack the time, patience, and willingness to look at things in a nonlinear way.

For example, Sargento Cheese Company, looking for other markets, analyzed the cheesecake market only to discover that the category was dominated by one manufacturer—Sara Lee.

The typical approach from that point on would have been attempting to make a cheesecake that is better tasting, has different flavors, comes in a different package, or is low in calories. However, with any one of those product adaptations, the company would have ended up competing with Sara Lee. A variety of other new product activities had led the company's new product operating team to examine the frozen novelty category.

The result was Montage™, Chocolate Covered Cheesecake-on-a-Stick. This product would not be positioned opposite the leader of the cheesecake category but, rather, would compete in the more fragmented frozen novelty category as a new-to-the-category product. The key to this example is the process that led the group to make associations from previously collected information, piece them together, and generate a new idea.

This new idea came about primarily because the company president had done four things:

⬥ Established a new product operating team made up of marketing, manufacturing, finance, sales, and research and development. He met bi-monthly with the team and also with individual members once a month for breakfast or lunch.

⬥ Hired from the outside a full-time new product development manager who reported directly to him.

⬥ Communicated frequently to the entire company and to the board of directors the role and importance of new products to the company's growth and, therefore, his total commitment to the new product program. Outside consultants had been brought in to help design the new product strategy, and several interactive meetings were held with all levels of management to garner commitment to the new product process.

⬥ Developed with the new product manager a strategic charter, financial goals, qualitative and quantitative screening criteria, and strategic roles for new products.

Thus, the president clearly demonstrated a strong commitment to new products. By establishing a separate department with a multidisciplinary team, clearly assigning responsibility for new products, and demonstrating a strong commitment, the company has provided itself with the means to generate the returns that they expect from new products.

But most companies don't. They talk about the importance of new products, but cut new product budgets to boost dividends, staff new product development departments with "creative types," and talk about how the lab technicians are developing exciting new products. Lab technicians alone, however, do not develop and commercialize successful new products. It takes a properly guided, motivated, and nurtured team.

So how can top management commitment be developed when it doesn't exist? Many managers feel powerless in this case. But how is gaining commitment behind new products any different from garnering support for a costly advertising campaign on an existing product? It requires the same political insight and internal sponsorship that is needed when managing upwards.

The point is to find a way to ignite some sparks of commitment from top management. The first step is to identify those who influence decisions of top management. Convincing and persuading them that new products are integral to the success of the company will begin the groundswell. New product awareness can also be built by having other functional and operating managers become spokespeople who point to the great need for new products in their own areas. Moreover, developing a game plan that top management signs off on is one of the most effective ways for increasing commitment, especially when top management reviews the plan often. Such reviews often serve as reminders of the commitment. In addition, a manager who calls the CEO on the phone and asks him or her out to lunch establishes an informal setting to begin the process of selling new product commitment.

I have seen few CEOs become born again new product zealots overnight. I have, however, seen top executives gradually increase their comfort with, and understanding of, the new product game and suddenly take a devoted stance on new products. Often a company will not realize for many months the transformation that has occurred. A CEO is not going to announce that he has finally seen the light. A CEO will establish a new product committee, begin allocating funds to previously poorly funded areas, and begin talking about new product objectives.

Top management must be willing to communicate its new product direction within the company. Then the new product development function can grow and mature in conjunction with top management's expectations. The new product manager or committee must establish a well-thought-out new product program. You cannot expect successful results in a few months. In a few years, however, if the setting and people are right, new products will begin to flow.

But what happens if top management is not committed to new products? While they can be gradually turned around over time, there are certain realistic limitations and constraints that must be lived with. However, let's examine a few ways that middle-level managers have effectively changed top management's perspectives and increased their level of commitment to new products:

- ✧ Nothing works better than a couple of new product successes. Sometimes it makes more sense to launch a couple of low-risk, me-too type new products to be able to demonstrate how the process can work. Simultaneously, however, top management must be receiving heavy doses of "New products is risky business." Without these constant admonishments, this approach can backfire. Top management becomes accustomed to successes and then is unwilling to accept a failure when it occurs. So the point of this approach is to build management's comfort with a few successes while "teaching" them about the failures that will ultimately be coming down the road.

- ✧ Another approach is to get top management more involved in the process. Ask members of top management to spend two days each month for the next three months assisting the new product team. If internally developed new products are important to the future earnings and revenue stream of the company, a total of six days a month is not asking too much. Then, ensure that top-management is exposed to prototype development, concept definition, screening, aspects of business analysis, a team meeting or two, and the like. The objective is to have top management gain a better understanding of the complexity of the process—and an appreciation for the multidisciplinary and multifunctional nature of managing new products.

✧ A third approach is to insist upon monthly status, update, or review meetings with top management. By establishing a formal two-to-three-hour monthly meeting, top management ends up being exposed to the process and to at least some of the risk elements. However, at these meetings the new product manager needs to solicit thinking from top management and not just spoon feed the accomplishments that have been made during the past month.

More latitude needs to be given to new product people. Yet, as already stressed, a structured process must provide the MAP to guide individual turns and twists in the road. There is a need for balanced, individual freedom matched to a systematic approach with obvious objectives. Management must be willing to bend the rules once in a while. They need to give enough autonomy to new product managers that they build ownership for new product objectives. They need to feel an emotional drive to get new products launched—not just another goal to meet. By providing new product managers with enough time, stability, and consistent funding, top management releases a flare that signals its intentions to support new products.

Innovation and creativity are interactive. They cannot come from a single individual. As a result, top management must be willing to commit the best people to the function. Often, al-

though a full-time new product manager may be assigned to
the new product activity, it is supported by a multifunctional
team of managers who spend only two half-days a week on
new products. The team's bosses see their responsibility as
managing the existing businesses—not developing new products. Consequently, working on new products for these team
members is not a priority—just one more thing to add to their
"to-do" lists. If top management is committed to new product
development, new product participants must have adequate
time to be involved in a substantive way. Again, it is not one
person who comes up with the new product of the decade.
Rather, it is a team that requires a time-committed and dedicated group of players.

In Summary

The elements involved in structuring and leading an effective
new product organization include:

- ✧ Creating the right environment
- ✧ Building new product teams and organizing according to a freestanding or a functionally-based
structure, determined by the types of new
products planned
- ✧ Establishing clear accountability, roles, and
responsibilities for "who does what" in the
process
- ✧ Positioning the new product function at the top
of the organization so that it reports directly to
senior management
- ✧ Getting the best people with the right skills to
lead, manage, and work on new products
- ✧ Sharing leadership for new product management
among participants in the process
- ✧ Fostering top-management commitment

10

Motivating and Rewarding Champions

I nnovation has become the industrial religion of the late 20th century. Business sees it as the key to increasing profits and market share. Governments automatically reach for it when trying to fix the economy. Around the world the rhetoric of innovation has replaced the post-war language of welfare economics. . . .

Two things set apart all organisations with a good record of innovation. One is that they foster individuals who are internally driven—whether they are motivated by money, power, fame or simply curiosity and the need for personal achievement. The second is that they do not leave innovation to chance. . . .

The Economist, "Industry Gets Religion," in A Survey of Innovation in Industry, February 20, 1999.

Free Balls and Missing Incentives

If you ever played pinball, you can remember what a great feeling it was to get a free ball after making a high enough score.

You may even have lost the game to another player, but somehow the *real* reward had already come—the free ball. Similarly, companies need to offer more "free balls" to new product participants. An individual manager may not win all the games or always have success with a new product, but if he or she shows enough skill and capability overall, a few free balls are indeed deserved. Free balls can come in the form of pats on the back, recognition from peers, funding for special ideas or projects, financial rewards, promotions, and even a "Thanks, you really did a great job." Free balls can be fairly inexpensive but can have a high-impact value, yet top management often rewards only the highest scorers—those at the very top of the company. Management does not take advantage of the power and motivating potential of free balls.

Most U.S. corporations are living in the Dark Ages in terms of motivating new product people through performance-based compensation and incentive systems. The majority of corporations are often afraid to take *any* risks when it comes to compensating a new product manager in ways other than traditionally accepted pay scales, point systems, and standardized job description-driven salary increases. Great strides appear to have been made in compensating CEOs through hefty bonus-reward structures that are tied to return on equity, stock appreciation, and other appropriate performance measures. However, top management apparently believe that they, themselves, are the only ones deserving of incentive systems that are tied to performance. Their bonuses are geared toward high return for high performance, so why can't new product people also get incentives that are based on actual performance of new products in the marketplace?

The most underdeveloped areas of new product management are effective financial rewards and incentive and compensation practices. Of even more concern, though, is that many corporate executives, compensation consultants, and the like, truly believe that their bonus systems are the *right* schemes for new product managers. One cause of this misconception is the fact that many personnel directors have no idea what skills are required to manage new products effectively, nor are they willing to rock the corporate boat by paying new product managers any differently from other senior people in the company. In their naiveté, they see little difference between the talent and skills required to run a day-to-day business and those required to run a new products program. It's no wonder that nothing has changed in the area of new product compensation practices. That's one of the major reasons the small business entrepreneurial phenomenon has taken off in recent years. The "serfs" no longer want the security and boring comfort of the "corporatocrasy." They want to take some risks and, be rewarded when their performance merits it—rewarded in a way commensurate with the result. Compensation programs that enable new product managers to get a piece of the action or invest their own equity in a new product would begin to simulate the entrepreneur's situation. Having your own cash invested in a project can often be a very effective motivator.

And yet corporate executives and human resource managers, for the most part, refuse to accept this idea. They are afraid that if you compensate new product personnel differently from operating managers, imbalances will result. Operating managers will see new product managers getting rewarded for their accomplishments and won't like it. But the inherent risk of achieving successful results with new products is usually far greater than the risk of managing an existing, business, even when the competition is intense. New product managers should be compensated in a way that addresses the risk and at the same time offers rewards for market-proven performance.

How is the entrepreneur rewarded? Financially, the rewards are tied directly to the bottom line of the income statement and equity value of the balance sheet. The entrepreneur cannot make a case for why he or she deserves a $25,000 bonus if there is only $5,000 left over in after-tax profit. There is no corporate coffer to run to. Entrepreneurs get paid according to how well they perform and what they deliver. Moreover, they are usually investing their own funds. Often hard-earned money is often put at total risk. Nothing motivates businesspeople more than the sight of dollars flowing out of their own wallets. It produces an electrical charge that sparks the entrepreneur into action. Suddenly, the projects that take months to finish in a large corporation are accomplished in weeks. Why can't the same stimulus that works for an entrepreneurial setting be instilled into a bureaucratic corporate setting? The fact is that it can: If top management is enlightened enough to see that different motivating techniques for new product managers can yield a high payout.

One of the problems, though, stems from the fact that any sound incentive system should have both a short- and long-term focus to it. Perhaps the payout to the new product team would not occur for three or four years. By that time, in many companies those same people would no longer even be in the new product area. They would have returned to their existing-business operating positions. Thus, a total change of culture is needed before altering the compensation practices of new product personnel. The first change requires an attitude that signals an acknowledgment by top management that new product personnel should be paid differently from operating managers. Next, and even more important, the corporate culture must instill credibility in the new products function. It must leave no doubt that it is a career path and that someone who stays in the new product area for five or six years is in a viable and progressive position, not a holding pattern waiting to get back to the mainstream. Third, new product people will need to make a commitment to work in new products for at least a three- to five-year time period. Without this type of willingness to persevere, long-term incentive programs will be meaningless and, therefore, provide no incremental motivation.

The Product Champion

Introducing change into an organization is difficult. New products represent significant change. They upset fixed routines, require the implementation of new procedures and methods and demand substantial nurturing time and energy. In reality, the new product process goes directly against the set schedules and bureaucracy of traditional organizations. It takes a special type of person to lead the development of a new product. It takes a "product champion" who can overcome the sluggish nature of the corporate organization by infusing entrepreneurial spirit into his or her efforts and the efforts of the group.

Product champions are managers who can integrate diverse

skills and focus the creative force of a small group toward the development and launch of a single product idea. They behave like entrepreneurs. Too often a new product concept dies because there was no sponsor behind it—no champion to direct it. The most important characteristic of product champions is that they are obsessed with the success of their product. They encourage experimentation, instill harmony, and build momentum in those who work with them. With their thorough knowledge of the market, the process, and the organization, they foster cooperation throughout the company. Overcoming internal resistance to a new product is another key job of a product champion. Internal selling of an idea is often as important as the external selling effort that comes later in the process. Without the support of many internal players, the result will be a lot of hard work with little return.

New champions can emerge from any level. Some CEOs who are very committed to new products serve as the occasional product champion. Consider, for example, Akio Morita, chairman of Sony, a committed proponent of new products, and a product champion. No one expected the Walkman to become the runaway success that it became. No one except Morita. From the start, he saw tremendous potential in the concept. He created and led a ten-member "Walkman team" to develop and guide the product's strategy. He turned the Walkman into a cooperative effort, spreading risk and cost across several Sony divisions. He insisted on a unified international marketing approach and on maintaining what consumers would consider a reasonable unit price, even if that meant running a deficit for several months after the launch. Morita's vision and commitment were the driving force behind the Walkman's quick introduction. The first sets were introduced less than one year after the conception of the idea. In its first seven years, the Walkman's success was proven—to the tune of ten million units sold.

The importance of a product champion to the overall success of new product development cannot be overstated. Almost half of the most successful companies encourage new product champions to promote and shepherd new product concepts through the development process. In fact, many companies depend on it. As the vice president of a consumer durables company put it, "The product champion facilitates change by accepting the personal risk and making a personal commitment." His counterpart at an industrial goods company agrees, "The product champion is a key element in our decision-making process. Without a sponsor, a new product concept will die. At least one person has to be enthusiastic about a concept to secure funding."

Analyze your own organizational structure relative to the type of new products being developed. The structure, support of top management, compensation practices, and leadership all interact to give companies the insight and the ability to manage innovation. Successful companies understand the true meaning of innovation. They realize the difference between maintenance, which generates today's profits to make tomorrow possible, and innovation, which investigates the source of tomorrow's profits. Successful companies have created the right environment, the right culture so that product champions are willing to accept the risk implicit in managing the new product process. They are willing to experiment, to learn, to change—and to fail. For in accepting the risks that accompany reward, they recognize the possibility of failure.

Career Risk in New Product Management

In most companies, there is minimal career risk in new products. Few managers have ever been fired for a new product failure. At times the risk is subtle. However, a manager who fails in new products may be moved to a lateral position to reside there for several years without promotion. But for the most part, companies neither reward nor penalize new product managers. No extremes exist—just mediocre, plain vanilla approaches to motivating new product people.

Well, it's time to reestablish the death penalty and the millionaire's club in corporations. A balance of rewards and penalties will stimulate an entrepreneurial environment more realistically. Entrepreneurs do not receive an annual 10 percent salary increase year after year regardless of their performance.

More often they hit it big one year and then make virtually nothing another year when high performance is not maintained. Bringing market reality and actual performance of new products back to new product managers' wallets may sharpen their entrepreneurial acumen.

Yet some companies do not consider new products to be any higher career risk for a manager than responsibility for an operating unit. A new product manager will screw up in the new product area and launch a bunch of failures, then get promoted because he or she has demonstrated a high degree of creativity and an ability to get new products into the marketplace, albeit failures. How stupid! Consider the signals that are sent out to the corporation—new products is an area where screwups are rewarded. So companies need to be careful to "unreward" people in the new product field for bad product performance just as they give high rewards for superior performance.

In actuality, the level of career risk *is* much higher for people involved in new products. A lack of results in new products is quite visible to top management. Unlike the regular business manager who achieves only 12 percent instead of the forecast 15 percent revenue objective, the new product manager who does not launch a new product has nothing to show for his or her efforts. Top management is rarely interested in the number of new product concepts in process. It wants to, and should, see results. Consequently, the new product manager has greater failure exposure.

The chance of a career setback or advancement impediment that new product people encounter is another risk that must be recognized by top management. However, if managers are encouraged and rewarded in a way that makes it pay for them to stay in the new product function for a three- to five-year period, the "don't stay out of the mainstream" syndrome will dissipate, and the function will be perceived as desirable.

While top management should always look for the best managers to fill every position, the reality is that there are usually only a handful of great business managers in any company. The new product area should get some of them if the role of new products in a company is an important one. Finding the best managers must underscore an approach to managing new products successfully. However, to attract the more risk-taking leaders most effective in new products, a greater *financial inducement is required*. The financial incentive needs to come up early on as well as later on in the process—both long- and short-term carrots are needed to provide a sustainable motivation to new product personnel.

To build an entrepreneurial environment, reinforce the importance of new products, and ensure that the best managers are attracted and committed to the new product effort, a bonus structure should be in place that recognizes the risks and rewards of successful new product performance.

Stimulating Risk-Taking

Managers' aversion to risk is understandable when one looks at the compensation practices of most companies. Most corporations tie compensation of its new product executives to a general performance evaluation: a base-salary increase and a semi-fixed bonus of some type. These practices force managers to focus on the bottom line, concentrating their efforts on short-term performance. With the reward systems currently in place, managers have no incentive to step out and take the risks inherent in and essential to innovative new products. It is simply not worth the risk. Their potential for reward is higher if they continue to introduce less risky, albeit less profitable, me-too products.

Adequate incentives for new product managers will be a cornerstone for developing successful new products in the future, yet very few companies currently tie compensation to actual new product performance even though this is exactly the kind of reward system that will breed success. One industrial-components president noted: "Compensation for new product managers is one of the key problems within our company. This year, for the first time, we have implemented a bonus system tied to long-term new product objectives."

In a successful consumer non-durables company, each new product manager works with a highly entrepreneurial-oriented reward system. At the end of three years, if the new product has achieved its original forecast goals, the managers receive 75 to 150 percent of their base salary as a bonus. If the product falls short of its targets, they get nothing. Obviously, sandbagging has to be guarded against, but the impetus for a successful new product launch far outweighs this potential danger.

Why pay managers in accordance with such irrelevant standards as the number of new products developed? The manager should be held accountable for the success of the new product, not just its introduction. Thus companies that reward risk taking and provide high upside returns for profitable new products will most likely end up in the winner's circle.

The benefits of rewarding risk taking are twofold. First, companies will be able to achieve the balance of high- and low-risk products needed to attain a portfolio of new product types that will provide some equilibrium to the risk equation. Second, incentive systems that reward success provide an enticement for new product managers to remain in the new product development function. Thus there is greater continuity in leadership, as managers are more likely to see long-term products through to commercialization. Tenured leadership also provides for the accumulation of new product experience—an important asset in the new product game.

Moreover, top management involvement in new products is required to let employees know that management is also sharing in the new product risks. This means that corporate managers need to leave their corner, glassed-in, ivory tower offices and move into the trenches with the people doing the work. The successful new product development programs—that is, the ones with the highest hit rates—belong to those companies that have a high degree of *top management support*: In other words, a top management team that fosters an entrepreneurial spirit by compensating employees involved in new products according to market performance. For example, a team of managers who are primarily responsible for the launch of a new product, which by end of the year 3 is generating $100,000 in net pre-tax profit and required only $45,000 in start-up costs, might each receive a $5,000 bonus. *Recognition* of some sort is the key.

New reward and incentive programs need to be designed to support and reinforce new product management. Currently, new product positions are not usually seen as long-term, career-advancing jobs. In order to ensure that strong professionals are attracted and committed to the new product effort, the compensation system must recognize the often high-risk status associated with new product work. Bonus systems, whether individual or group, should be created to reward all members that are associated with new product successes.

New Product Compensation Programs

An incentive system may be based on a percentage of profits generated from new products or even phantom stock ownership in a new product line, but the key is to tie the reward system to actual market performance. Thus, if all of the new products bomb during a five-year period, then there will be *no* bonuses or rewards for the new product team. "That's not fair," whines the risk-averse corporate bureaucrat. No: That's the downside risk that must accompany a performance-based incentive system.

On the other hand, when the new products launched during the same period end up dropping $4 million in profits to the corporate bottom line and ten new product people get a $50,000 bonus, the perspective on what's fair and what's not will suddenly change. Obviously, the type of person who is content with a virtually guaranteed 5 percent base salary increase and a bonus based on 15 percent of salary will not be willing to move into a performance-driven compensation plan.

Another problem that is often brought up by naysaying managers when they discuss paying on performance is the lack of control that new product managers have over the success of a new product. Is it really the new product team's fault if the sales force does a rotten job of selling, or if competition reduces the price and substantially cuts demand for the new product just launched? It sure is the fault of the new product team. Developing a mock-up prototype is not the only activity involved in managing new products successfully. The process calls for taking an idea from the concept stage all the way to commercialization. This final stage includes motivating the sales force to do the proper sell-in. The business-analysis stage includes examining potential competitive responses, and therefore a contingency plan should have been developed to counteract the competitor's price decrease. Look, we can develop a list a mile long of all the external and internal factors that are not under the direct control of new product managers. And all of these factors can destroy even the best and most innovative new product. But survival of the fittest reigns. If new product people get rewarded on market performance, then they need to manage the entire process. That means taking the responsibility for effective launch and support programs, not just grinding through a bunch of prototypes that are turned over to marketing to do with as they please.

Developing new products is a totally different business function from day-to-day product line and business management. It calls for different skills, different performance measures, different types of risk-taking individuals, and as a result, different compensation and incentive plans. A Midwest industrial products company, nearly $300 million in sales, paid over $500,000 in bonus money to six new product managers in two years. The managers' bonuses exceeded their base salaries. And what had the company received in return? During the previous three years, this group had launched fifteen new products that by year three were generating $60 million in incremental revenues and dropping $4.5 million in incremental profits to the bottom line. So the company paid out $.5 million to the people who had provided the corporation with a net increase of $4 million in profits. Not a bad deal. But the point is that it was a great deal for the company *and* the new product team. Both were rewarded. Both were motivated.

Blank stares filled the room after I had recommended to the top management of a $5 billion corporation that the new product directors should have a bonus program tied directly to performance of new products in the marketplace. When I described the program in more detail, top management suddenly realized that if new products really succeeded and did extremely well, the new product director's bonuses would be more than the divisional president's bonus. Of course, they said this bonus system just would not work. However, within a few months, they decided to *test* a new incentive system for

one division. The system linked bonuses to new products. To
date five new-to-the-company products have been launched,
contributing over $40 million in revenues. The test is being
continued.

Compensation practices are one area, in particular, where
large corporations can learn from small entrepreneurial companies. Why are the incentive systems so demonstrably different? Corporate policies driven by staffers rather than managers
are eating away at any remains of entrepreneurial attitude in
corporations.

Corporations' incentive systems should embody some of the
same characteristics of an entrepreneurial environment, for
example:

- ◇ Phantom stock investment: New product managers
  can buy stock options of a new product prior to commercialization. Up to 10 percent of the "stock" can be
  purchased. The purchase price might be set by total
  development, capital, and launch costs. Thus, if
  $800,000 were the "purchase price," a 2 percent own-
  ership would cost an internal investor $16,000.
  Therefore, if the new product averages $500,000 in
  net profits during the next five years, the investor's
  return during that time would be 2 percent of $2.5
  million, or $50,000. On the other hand, if the new
  product generates a cumulative five-year profit of
  $300,000, the investor's return will be only $6,000,
  representing a $10,000 loss.

- ◇ Long-range bonus program: A new product manager
  would receive a bonus in the third, fourth, and fifth
  years based on the performance of new products
  launched during the first two years. The bonus
  might be based on a percentage of total cumulative
  profits generated from the new product introductions. Of course, if the manager continued to stay in
  the new products area beyond the five years, new
  products launched in year 3 would be compensated
  for in year 6.

Any type of reward system that fosters an entrepreneurial, risk-taking environment to motivate managers is the real answer—not size of office and 5 percent annual base-salary increases. The best approach to people management is to find out their unique needs and desires, find a way to match those to the company's goals, and develop a bonus system that will measure and reward performance.

Teams can be rewarded as well as individuals. Is there any reason why a five-person new product team working on three new-to-the-world products should not be able to invest $10,000 each in these new products and buy a small portion of the product's "equity"? The level of motivation, dedication, and perseverance to make those new products succeed will be substantially increased by the new product "investors" involved. Let employees share in the risk and the returns. It's time for U.S. corporations to adopt some of the practices of small entrepreneurial companies, using financial rewards to motivate managers.

For example, one compensation plan that has had strong results in a consumer durables company is an incentive system in which two overlapping bonus programs are in place for the six key managers in the new business development area of their $400 million division.

First, there is a long-term bonus that is directly tied to actual external market performance of new products.

Second, there is a short-term bonus based on internal performance of successful management of the new product process.

The long-term bonus program is initiated one year after commercialization of the group's first new product. Thus, if the first new product does not get out the door until the end of the second year, it will take a minimum of three years for the long-term bonus to even begin to be activated. Once the program is underway, the bonuses will be paid annually based directly on the performance of the new product in the marketplace, for as long as the people receiving them remain in the new product area. As a result, new product managers have the opportunity to earn as much as 50 percent of their annual base salary in bonus rewards if the new product's market performance matches or exceeds pre-commercialization financial targets. Of course, with this type of program, one that is based on achievement of new product financial targets, you have to beware of low-ball forecasting. New product projections could end up being "sandbagged" in order to meet bonus award targets. However, the checks and balances in this approach are such that if the projections are too low, top management will probably not approve the launch of the project anyway. Moreover, with top management involved in the approval process, the chances are few that the projections will be totally unrealistic.

Let's examine how a long-term bonus payout might work. In years 1 and 2 there would be no bonus payout at all. The first new product was launched at the end of the first year, with the bonus program starting up the end of the second year. By year 3 only five new products had been launched, one fewer than the objective of six, and revenues were at $2 million rather than the forecast $3 million. No bonus. So close and yet no cigar. That's just the way this bonus system works: you either make it or you don't.

However, in year 4 new product revenues exceeded the goal of $14 million by $2 million. Thus, these $75,000 managers were awarded $37,000 bonuses. In fact, for the next two years they continued to receive roughly $40,000 in bonuses, because the new product objectives were being consistently met. By the end of the sixth year, each new product manager had received $115,000 in bonus money. In contrast, a more conservative annual bonus program based on 15 percent of base would have resulted in a cumulative payout during that five-year period of roughly $56,000. However, keep in mind that these new product managers did not receive anything in the first three years. Under the more conservative program, they would have received $33,750 during the first three years.

Now with the above example an additional short-term bonus might represent an upside of 20 percent of base salary annually and would be aimed more toward internal performance in terms of how well the process was managed. It might be based on the number of new products by type that made it to different stages of the development process and adherence to timetables and budgets set for approved projects. So there is a buffer against the three-year wait for a long-term bonus. And there should be. This short-term bonus, if performance meets expectations, should accommodate the inherent risk of taking the leap to the new product side of a corporation.

Finally, beyond the six new product managers who participate in this long- and short-term bonus program, the division provides annual cash awards to people who have made significant contributions to the overall success of the new product program or specific contributions to individual new product concepts. A $1,500 bonus is awarded to all team members from all functional areas involved with the development of the top three new products introduced each year. There is an additional reward of $2,000 to the five managers from any function who contribute the most to moving new products through the process effectively.

These awards help to build a team-oriented environment. The major benefit is that they send a signal throughout the company: new products are important. You can be an active participant in the process, regardless of your functional responsibility. They also recognize the efforts of people who do not have direct responsibility for new products. They show that managing new products is a multidisciplinary process that requires the services of numerous functional managers during the development of the new product concept.

Another example of a longer-term compensation program that is tied to new product performance is illustrated by a smaller $150 million company. There are three key new product people: a new product director, a research-and-development director, and an engineering director. These three people devote 100 percent of their time to new product development. Their compensation program includes a bonus payout that is based on pre-tax operating income generated from each new product. They receive, collectively, up to 10 percent of total annual pre-tax operating income from all of the new products they develop. As a result, these three managers each received zero cash in the first two years, a $6,000 bonus in year 3, a $95,000 bonus in year 4, a $125,000 bonus in year 5, and a $145,000 bonus in year 6. Were they motivated? Yes! By year 5 the new products that had been launched during the five-year time period were generating $45 million in incremental revenue and over $2 million in after-tax profits.

At 3M there are two internal ventures for employees: the Alpha Program and the Genesis Program. Both "venture funds" are aimed at building more innovation and entrepreneurship into the company. These corporate funds are aimed at encouraging individual entrepreneurship to shine through corporate shadows. The Genesis Program is for people who have a technological or process oriented idea they would like to pursue. If funding is provided to the individual, then for a given period of time, he or she is able to spend time developing the idea. While the entire corporation instills a sense of urgency and importance on new products, not all good ideas can be pursued at once. Divisions have varying priorities and different time-tables. These corporate programs are intended to make people feel that even if their division does not currently have the time or resources to support these efforts, the parent company will provide permission to develop it. The Alpha Program is similar in nature but is aimed at innovative ideas within the company, for instance, a new idea for information transferring, communication linking, cost savings in the area of word processing, or a new business opportunity.

The real benefit of these two programs is the internal message that is sent out to all 70,000 3M employees: Whoever and wherever you are, we at the corporate level are interested in listening to and possibly funding your own individual ideas. It is a powerful message that may indeed work to further instill an entrepreneurial spirit into the company.

In companies that allow a great deal of entrepreneurial activity, one of the most important factors in building an innovative mindset is the green light that managers give for individual projects. The perception becomes, "If top management says that's a good idea, we trust your judgment and respect your intuition on this. Therefore, we'll fund your pursuit of it." It is the free-ball phenomenon. That is, even though you may not win the next game, you're rewarded with a free ball. Wow! is the usual response to this type of corporate communication. The motivating benefit is the recognition that it fosters. Employees begin to believe that it is worth it to be creative and innovative. It is not the bonus nor even the funding. It is the personal recognition. By supporting individual ideas, management can bring an entire culture into focus, centering on the emotional and psychological rewards that come from recognizing individuals as valuable "assets" to the corporation.

While inspiring teamwork is an important part of the success equation, equally as paramount is the need to recognize and support the emotional needs of new product players. Yet so often senior managers see new products as a soft, mushy area that they would prefer not to deal with. The macho attitude toward managing people continues to dominate many management styles. Consequently, how can managers justify sensitivity? They think that they may be taken advantage of if they show a human side. Stay tough and rough is the motto— for the losers of the future.

The successful new product companies are those that invest in people as well as projects. Demonstrating a desire to invest in human resources suggests the value that management places on the contributions that its people rather than plants, computers, or systems can provide. When employees feel that they are the integral cogs of the development wheel, they tend to act more quickly and consistently.

The overall results when innovation takes hold may be invisible or, at least, immeasurable for many years. Managers have to be rewarded for risk taking. Otherwise, they soon realize that their rewards are based on a predetermined point system that only perpetuates corporate mediocrity and apathy.

Managers should be rewarded based on the performance of a new product in the marketplace—without ceilings and percentage increase maximums. The fact is, however, that instead of receiving $75,000 bonuses for developing a successful $5 million new product that generates 20 percent pre-tax margins by the end of the year 2, most managers will get the corporate "golden goose" award, a pat on the back, and another 8 or 10 percent annual salary boost.

Thus, as managers begin to mature in the corporate arena, they see that the only way to escape the imprisoning and inevitable annual salary increase is to get promoted or create a job that will require a new job description and reclassification of compensation points. As a result, corporate new product queues fill up with a proliferation of line extensions, flankers, and new and improved versions of old products.

"Why risk a new product introduction that could hurt the near-term earnings stream?" Of course, dividends and increases in shareholder wealth are the ultimate objective of any corporation but short- and long-term tradeoffs need to be balanced. Successful new products do propel stock prices. The corporate engines need fuel that comes from innovative products. It's time to fire up conservative managers by breathing an entrepreneurial spirit into their lungs.

Setting A Management Style of Disciplined Freedom

Giving individuals who are involved in the new product function the latitude and room to breathe often breeds a greater degree of innovation. But there must be a balance between structure and flexibility; creativity and analytics; teamwork and individual accomplishment.

That is why I have coined the term *disciplined freedom* to describe the management style or culture that provides a balance whereby individuals have a sense of entrepreneurship and creativity and receive enough direction and control to guide their efforts. Achieving this balance is a very delicate and difficult task for the new product leader who is trying to instill in the people that work with him or her an attitude that embodies flexibility with structure. Creativity requires training, a problem-solving focus, and a blend of feeling and thinking. Visions need to be guided: Market information and business analysis provides a check on creative vision making and often stimulates creativity further.

Perhaps a good way to think about disciplined freedom is by examining Jean Piaget, the twentieth-century educator who spent his life studying how children and adults learn. His own observations led him to the belief that children who experienced play and learning as *one* were better able to develop. Piaget perceived that the recall and repetition exercises prevalent in most school systems were the totally wrong approach.

All that was being accomplished was an ability to remember and recall, not an ability to think independently, creatively, or intuitively. How can creativity or intuition be developed in a child if the only "learning" that takes place is repeating what the teacher has already recited? That is not unlike some companies where managers introduce low-risk new products that echo what top management has recited: "We don't want any new product failures."

Unfortunately, many corporate managers do not nurture creative, independent managers. Instead, they breed mindless nomads who wander the corporate corridors reciting things they know will be well received by peers and superiors. Like the pupil who gets a gold star because she spells and recites all the words correctly, the manager who is typically rewarded in a company is the one who has been a "prudent and pragmatic" business manager. What they really mean is that the person who does not rock the boat, take risks, express emotion, or demonstrate any guts is the one who ultimately will rise to the top. Many successful CEOs have indeed been able to achieve commendable results through regimented management styles. But the question remains: How much more would their companies have grown if they had been willing to take more risks and instill in their management a feeling that failing is acceptable, that mistakes are okay?

In a corporate culture that embodies the beliefs of Piaget, new product participants enjoy the process of new product development. The more they do, the more they learn, and the more they learn, the more successes they enjoy. That builds self-confidence and means more active listening, cooperative interplay with other functions, and a willingness to take risks. Managers are encouraged to think and act creatively and individualistically. That spells a productive and usually profitable new product program.

Hearing a CEO for a consumer-packaged-goods company talk about his attitudes on risk taking suggests an understanding of, and sensitivity to, the inherent risk-return nature of new products. However, listening to his managers we hear a different point of view: John accepts the results of any new product as long as it is not a failure—failure is not part of his vocabulary.

Being truly committed to new products takes guts. It requires a constant blend of tenacity and optimism. It takes a mixture of disciplined freedom, active listening, and sensitivity to the difficulty and riskiness of developing new products. A Piagetian perspective on new product management suggests the ability to allow managers to think for themselves—to expect something other than the pat answer; the one that *should* be made rather than the one that is "expected" to be made. It suggests an environment that respects the views and ideas of everyone in the group. And collectively, the group fosters a vibrant and dynamic team of intuitive, risk-taking entrepreneurs.

Getting A Small-Company Feel

One key attribute that needs to be instilled in a new product team is a small-company feel—a climate that makes individuals feel as if there is some room to move, to try some dead-end paths, and to make some mistakes. The small-company feel also involves making managers feel as if they have some stake in the wins and the losses. So reward structures that provide a high upside for the successes, and at the same time a downside for the failures help to encourage managers to simulate an entrepreneurial environment.

In innovating companies, a number of aspects of the organization's culture and structure provide new product "power"—i.e., market information, human resources, dedicated time, developmental funds, and capital investments. A new product manager should not have to be constantly "tin-cupping" it through the corporate hallways and management offices to get funding and people to help out with new products. A sign of new product commitment is having these resources in place so that a new product manager can focus time and attention on how best to manage and utilize these resources rather than trying to figure out ways to secure them. Then again, "power" must be pursued in a corporation as well as made available. A certain degree of struggle is usually necessary to get the requisite resources.

An important lesson to be learned from entrepreneurs is that they are typically willing to *apply* what they have learned in the past to new situations—even though the situations may be totally new. Past experience and performance do not restrain the direction and degree of risk taken in the future. Instead, previous experience is used as the building blocks—cornerstones put into place when it's time to erect the next new venture. They quickly learn that their most valuable and trusted resource is themselves. Therefore, a sense of self-worth develops quickly, and performance usually does improve. It is regaining some of *these* values in corporations that is so desperately needed not only for new product management but also for general management.

The environment, more than any one person, makes the biggest difference in building a successful new product team. And that is a job for top management. Top management can make or break a successful new product program. It's as simple as that. Of course, even with top-management commitment, many other variables are needed; but without it, the best strategy, process, organization, and resource base will have an uphill battle, similar to the struggle of Sisyphus, the cruel mythical king who was condemned forever to roll a huge stone up a hill only to have it roll down again upon nearing the top.

Building sponsors or product champions is a key technique of effectively managed new product companies. Most companies recognize that a new product doesn't get commercialized unless someone is personally interested in it. The best way to generate product champions is to recognize and reward any that may already exist. Once others in the company understand that sponsorship of a product is an accepted and encouraged form of behavior, there is a greater chance that additional champions will pop up. Moreover, the signal should be clearly communicated to new product participants that champions are the lifeblood of any new product program. At the same time, the more subtle, thoughtful, yet effective manager should in no way be misled into believing that he needs to "beat his chest" before he will be recognized as a productive and effective new product manager. A balance is needed. Too often, the person who is overly demonstrative in his or her enthusiasm for a product is perceived as an airhead, and therefore loses ground, decision-making power, and executive effectiveness.

Delegating more responsibility and allowing more individualistic decision making are both catalysts in ferreting out new product champions. As long as a certain degree of freedom is perceived, the new product players will be more inclined to stand up for their product, knowing that management will support their future decisions. And now there is enough latitude for the driver to take a variety of paths, but eventually he or she will arrive at the scheduled destination.

Companies sometimes make the mistake of trying to balance a sense of urgency and timeliness of new product launches with short-term productivity shortcuts. Doing the right amount of homework on a category and spending more time on consumer testing and business analysis for a new concept are essential components of the process. As a result, they are not inefficient time spenders but rather, in the long run, time savers. On the other hand, a new product concept can be tested and analyzed to death, or remain in a test market for so long that consumer trends shift or competition beats you to the draw. While a sense of urgency is a vital attribute of any new product group, priorities must be set to identify those parts of the process that will remain sacred. It requires a new product manager or coordinator to stay on top of the situation and carefully monitor the progression of each new product's trip down the road to commercialization.

The most frequently cited tools to be mentioned when new product managers are asked what can have the greatest impact on new product success are: time, the right mix of people, top management support, decision-making autonomy, and information. Interestingly, capital and financial funding are not mentioned as the most common impediments to success.

This implies that the culture—the environment and tone that top managers set for new products—is the underlying key to establishing a committed team of players who are focused and driven to get new products out the door. Time seems to be the most difficult resource to secure and manage, especially when it is the time of functional managers. The existing business brush fires end up getting the bulk of the attention. Thus, management must communicate to all senior and middle managers the need to allocate time to new products—and plan for it—not just react to deadlines and missed schedules. Resource dilution is a sure-fire way to reach instant mediocrity.

The first rule is constant demonstration of commitment; the second rule is appreciation, understanding, and recognition of good performers. Employees are rarely thanked enough for their accomplishments. Usually, management takes the attitude that whatever they achieve is just part of the job: "They get paid to do that." Yet motivating people to great heights produces better results and more effective use of time. Doing enough homework early on often provides greater lead-time later in the process. A quick market launch may be all the competitive advantage needed, in some cases to preempt a competitive entry and establish your product in the consumer's mind.

Even though executives can verbally support innovation, some in effect resist it by attempting to match unrealistic objectives and expectations with insufficient resources. It becomes a no-win situation for the new product participants. With minimal resources, there can be only minimal progress and little hope that additional doses of creativity will be appreciated. The worst situation occurs when top management constantly vascillates in its support for new products. Priorities shift, and two years later management does not understand why nothing has been accomplished in the new product area.

In Summary

People have to be encouraged to integrate information, intuition, and instinct. To a great extent, the issue is not the invention of new tools and approaches to developing new products. It is a matter of utilizing the existing resource base and existing internal tools.

It does not take long for others to follow and adopt the newly accepted behavioral patterns. This suggests that leadership matters. A series of small changes by a few people can translate quickly into a major attitude and cultural change throughout a company.

Rewarding and motivating product champions must be based on programs that demonstrate to the organization that new product success really matters—as much as or more than virtually any other corporate objective. Stimulating risk taking and balancing short- and long-term incentives will move a company more toward a small-company, entrepreneurial culture. New types of financial rewards need to be developed to motivate individuals and new product teams.

CHAPTER 11

Attitude: Creating the Culture

> T*he trouble is that you can't suddenly start experimenting when you realize you're in trouble unless you've been experimenting all along. It's too late once things have changed in your core business. Ideally, you should have experimented with new products, technologies, channels, promotions all along. Then, when you sense that 'something has changed,' you will have a number of experiments that can be relied upon. . . .*

Andrew Grove (President and CEO, Intel), *Only the Paranoid Survive* (New York: Doubleday, 1996), p. 130.

Attitude and mindset are the be-all and end-all for creating a truly innovative company. Attitude shapes culture, and culture embraces or rejects innovation. It's quite clear; distinct. There is very little "gray." A company creates a culture that either reinforces and encourages risk-taking or perpetuates low self-esteem and high risk-aversion.

The MAP System™ simply can not work well on an ongoing basis without attitude and culture providing the glue to hold all the components together. Attitude makes or breaks culture, and culture impedes or accelerates the success of the MAP System™.

Crafting a culture that enables *everyone* within a company to feel and be innovative is probably the most important task for all senior executives in the 21st century. We've moved too far as a business society in believing that technologies, processes, the internet, etc., are *more* valuable than a company's people. However, they are the assets we should value the most.

The MAP System™ is based on seven interdependent and virtually interconnected components. Successful innovation occurs when people are managed, motivated, and measured in a way that leverages a plan and process to foster an attitude and culture that encourages risk-taking, open communication, and *trust* among employees and managers.

What is Culture?

According to the dictionary, culture is "the sum total of the attainments and learned behavior patterns of a specific period or people."

In our book, *Values-Based Leadership*, my wife and I describe culture as:

> A state-of-mind that gets translated into a set of actions, communications, and responses. It is a series of human signals that include verbal, physical and emotional signs. Culture therefore resides in our brains, which are frequently deciphering the signals we receive daily from others.

Of course, culture is perpetuated by the way(s) each person interprets the signals and responds to them in an integrative manner. Thus, culture involves developing and sharing a common set of beliefs, norms, attitudes and goals. Cultures can be created consciously and deliberately, but too often they develop unconsciously without a concerted effort or focused vision for what employees and managers want the culture to become. In short, culture is something that is carried around in our heads. This is why it is so difficult to change a company's culture. The norms and values that exist in the workplace are shared among each other. In turn, mindsets and attitudes are formed and reformed. According to Kotter and Heskett (1991), "Culture is an interdependent set of beliefs, values, ways of behaving, and tools for living that are so common in a community that they tend to perpetuate themselves. These values persist over time even when the group changes."

Caring for others is an aspect of an innovative culture that is most often missing from the contemporary workplace. Letting people know that their co-workers do care for them automatically increases their self-esteem. This provides more intrinsic security and a stronger sense of self. In short, a culture that builds the self-esteem of each individual will be a formidable company—a productive place where innovation will flourish. Innovative attitudes and mindsets give people permission to take risks, make mistakes, and be free yet at the same time accountable for tangible results.

The Role of Attitude and Culture

The primary reason for creating a culture of innovation is economic. Margins increase, customers buy more, earnings increase, and stock prices greatly appreciate. Employees feel that they are part of a winning team. Firms that cater to innovation are by far the best performing and most profitable.

Newness provides high returns. Companies that foster an innovative culture are more apt to exceed goals and deliver higher revenues to shareholders. The "Survey of Innovation in Industry," published by *The Economist* (2/20/99), states: "Two things set apart all organizations with a good record of innovation. One is that they foster individuals who are internally driven . . . the second is that they do not leave innovation to chance; they pursue it systematically." The survey goes on to state that breakthrough innovations usually come from a fundamental "rethink," not from listening to big customers. Quite often they stem from individual engineers who refuse to abandon a pet idea. Although innovations cannot be made to order, *The Economist* states, companies can do the next best thing: encourage the right conditions to allow radical ideas to be developed.

A four-year research project, conducted by John Kotter and James Heskett on corporate cultures, shows that firms which emphasize customers, stockholders and employees financially outperformed firms that did not have those traits by huge margins. Other findings from the study include:

- ✧ Corporate culture will probably be an even more important factor in determining the success or failure of firms in the next decade.

- ✧ Corporate cultures that inhibit strong long-term financial performance are not rare; they develop easily, even in firms that are full of reasonable and intelligent people. Once these exist, they are extremely difficult to change.

- ✧ Although tough to change, corporate cultures can be made more performance enhancing. This is complex and takes time.

A 1998 survey of the world's leading 300 international companies, sponsored by the Department of Trade and Industry in Britain, found that countries that sustained lots of competitive and innovative firms were better at churning out well-trained young people with all the skills their industries required. ("Survey of Innovation in Industry," *The Economist* 2/20/99)

The *Economist Intelligence* researched 15 companies for their CEO Roundtable and found that all were focused on reducing costs. They looked at every functional area and found that the savings were accomplished by technology upgrading, reduced production costs, and integrated supply-chain management. But what distinguished the better performers is that they are "learning organizations." Their CEOs created a learning culture, encouraged innovation and new ideas. (*The Economic Times*, 10/28/99).

Then there is 3M, a classic example of a company that continuously achieves higher- than- anticipated revenues by fostering innovation. A fourth of its annual revenue comes from products less than five years old. Innovation is strategically built into 3M's culture by giving employees time to create and money to execute.

According to Kuczmarski & Associates' "Winning New Product and Service Practices for the 1990's" survey, the most crucial ingredient in the new product and service formula is people. Nearly 85% of respondents prefer recognition or augmented job responsibility to motivate new product and service professionals:

> More than anything, it is this "fifth wave" of industrial innovation that lies behind America's extraordinary resurgence in the 1990s. This flow of new products, processes, opportunities and jobs which started in America a decade ago is now turning into a full-scale industrial revolution. . . . Where productivity growth [in the states] used to be well below 1% a year, since 1992 the rate of increase has mostly been much higher, up to 3% a year. A large chunk of that growth seems to originate in the wave of innovation now sweeping America." (*The Economist*, 2/20/99)

It would sure be a lot easier to create a plan or process—both are tangible and definable—than try to create an amorphous and ever-changing culture that stimulates and energizes innovations. Attitude and culture enable the plan, process, and people to function harmoniously and synergistically with each other. Attitude, in particular, becomes the inner psyche of the culture. The way people talk, think, and behave is impacted greatly by culture.

In order to be creative, insightful, and inspired to develop new ideas and push concepts to launch, we need to feel good about ourselves. We need to be our own person—to be able to act in a way that is true to our being. If the culture we work in dictates how to communicate and behave, it will be very difficult to be innovative. As Nathaniel Branden states in his book, *Self-Esteem at Work,* "An overly conformist business culture is deadly to the innovator. Creative and innovative people tend to manifest significant autonomy and independence. Creativity does not like to take orders."

Interestingly, few employees anywhere want to feel that they must tightly conform to rules, regulations, and corporate policies. While it's fine to establish corporate "rules of the road" to live by, each individual needs to feel a sense of freedom, control, and self-worth.

The bottom line for innovative people is that they are driven far more by intrinsic motivation rather than by external motivators. Intrinsic motivation fuels self-actualization. As a being, I feel a greater sense of self-pride and ego satisfaction by creating and launching new things. Ultimately, the most powerful intrinsic motivation is achieving goals and exceeding expectations in a way that makes us elevate our self-worth and self-esteem. Self-confidence comes from higher self-esteem. And higher self-confidence yields a strong sense of personal enrichment that produces innovative thinking and actions.

When a culture has been created that enables co-workers to trust each other, respect each other, and convey genuine concern for and interest in each other, you'll have dynamic innovation. The number and quality of innovations will soar, the growth rates achieved from new products and services will far surpass even the most aggressive stretch goals, and your stock price will double, triple, or quadruple every year or so. Employees will feel good about themselves, more innovations will materialize, and the MAP System™ will be operating at full steam.

But it all stems from creating the right culture.

How Can an Innovation Culture Be Created?

You create an innovation culture by behaving and talking to employees and managers as if each person was the only employee you had. You make sure that each person sees how valuable they are to the company overall.

You can recognize a company with an innovation mindset by the way employees interact with each other. They treat each other with respect, admiration, and cooperation. They smile. They laugh. They express consideration and thoughtfulness for each other. They listen. They focus on the benefits desired by consumers rather than on their own personal gain. They come to work with an optimistic enthusiasm because they believe that what they do each day really does count. They focus on the future rather than on the past. They exude self-confidence, possess a healthy self-esteem, and believe in their own capabilities and strengths. They have faith in innovation and in each other.

An innovation culture expresses attitudes that should be adopted throughout an organization by virtually every employee—from the CEO to the hourly worker. While a mindset has to exist in individuals, it can spread and be adopted and nurtured by others. It is a pervasive aura that has a spirit of its own. This mindset stimulates and motivates individual employees, as well as teams, to holistically endorse a belief in creating newness.

Harvard professor, Teresa M. Amabile is a leading expert on inspiring creativity within a company's culture. She has been researching the topic for over 20 years and has done numerous studies on the impact of a company's culture on the bottom line. She defines business creativity as an idea that is not only original, but also appropriate, useful and actionable. It must somehow influence the way business gets done. She states that there are three components to creativity:

- ✧ Expertise which equals knowledge (technical, procedural, and intellectual).
- ✧ Creative thinking skills that determine how flexibly and imaginatively people approach problems.
- ✧ Motivation—an inner passion to solve the problem at hand leads to solutions far more effectively than the use of external rewards, such as money.

It is important to note that there are two kinds of motivation: extrinsic and intrinsic, the latter being far more essential for creativity. Extrinsic motivation comes from outside a person—

a carrot or a stick, money or a promotion. But passion and in-terest—a person's internal desire to do something—are what intrinsic motivation is all about. When people are intrinsically motivated, they engage in their work for the challenge and en-joyment of it.

Intrinsic motivation can be increased considerably by even subtle changes in an organization's environment. When it comes to powerful innovators, they should know that those things that affect intrinsic motivation would yield more imme-diate results.

Dorothy Leonard-Barton states in her book *Wellsprings of Knowledge* that firms are knowledge as well as financial insti-tutions. Companies, like individuals, compete on the basis of their ability to create and utilize knowledge. By properly dis-seminating today's knowledge among all employees, this knowledge will turn into tomorrow's capabilities.

In many places, including in this book, one can find refer-ences to businesses as "learning environments." The concept of creating a learning environment parallels Teresa Amabile's contention that intrinsic motivation is among one of the best ways to motivate employees and thus spur an innovative com-pany culture. If employees are continuously learning and being "stretched," they will be more passionate about and take own-ership of their work.

Chaparral Steel is a great example of how to create this kind of environment in the way that it fosters knowledge-sharing among employees. Chaparral Steel is the 10th largest US Steel producer. CEO Gordon Forward sees his company's culture as a learning organization. . . . "One of our core competencies is the rapid realization of new technology into [steel] products." While they have won numerous awards and have the fastest production time in the industry, they have chosen not to pur-sue expansion, due in large part, to a deep concern for retain-ing the culture.

Lucent is another great example of how to encourage idea generation and risk taking. Any Lucent employee can come to Mr. Thomas Uhlman, head of Lucent's New Ventures Group, with a bright idea. If it passes, his group will provide seed money so a business plan can be put together. If that looks promising, larger chunks of money are made available to develop a working prototype and do market research. Researchers get phantom shares in their new enterprise while continuing to draw salaries from Lucent.

The Spirit of Risk-Taking

Defining risk-taking is difficult because it can mean many things to many people. However, certain initiatives "make up" or help to create a risk-taking culture. These include building self-esteem, empowering employees, and rewarding initiative.

Ian C. MacMillian describes his theory of "Internal Venturing" in his book *"Corporate Venturing: Creating New Business Within the Firm."* Internal venturing is the idea of stimulating high-risk activities that generate new businesses.

Successful managers take "opportunity risks" which emphasize innovation, initiative and entrepreneurship. Many experts believe that taking too little risk can be as bad as taking too much. Because most experts agree that there is no right formula for creating an entrepreneurial spirit, it is best to learn by example.

L.D. De Simone, Chairman and CEO, 3M. "Our corporate policies and procedures genuinely promote personal freedom. We have a well-known guideline—unwritten but universally understood— that our 8,000 researchers can spend 15% of their time working on an idea without approval from management. . . .

"Supporting entrepreneurial activity depends heavily on management's ability to trust people . . . we don't expect success every time, but we do expect our researchers to learn from their failures . . . as long as they are able to pour new ideas into the top of the funnel, we know that we'll get new products at the bottom." He goes on to state that they have incorporated criteria and questions into their interviewing process to ensure they are hiring innovators. He says innovators are inquisitive, passionate, and self-starting."

Bill Harris, Executive Vice President, Intuit. "[Because of Intuit's rapid growth] we needed a new structure that would allow the people directly involved in a project to make decisions quickly. When our new CEO arrived last year to help manage the company's growth, he decided to bust the organization apart. He created eight separate business units, each with its own general manager and customer mission. The basic goals were to flatten the organization and fragment the decision-making process. Today . . . decisions are left to the business units—and within those units, they are usually left to the individual product teams."

"We believe that fragmenting the company into small decision-making divisions has been a vital first step, but it can take us only part of the way toward building a customer-centered organization. To be truly entrepreneurial, we must encourage and allow our people—at all levels—to respond completely and immediately to our customers. Not only is this the source of great customer service, it's also crucial for sustained innovation. At Intuit, we regularly invest $1/3$ to $1/2$ our operating income in new products.

"Innovation is a risky business, and failure is commonplace. Rewarding success is easy, but we think that rewarding intelligent failure is more important. We don't judge people strictly on results, we try to judge them by the quality of their efforts. We want people to take intelligent business risks without also risking their careers."

Charles P. Holt, Vice President of the Wilson Center for Research and Technology, Xerox. "If innovation is the ability to recognize opportunity, then the essence of being an entrepreneur is being able to mobilize talent and resources quickly to seize that opportunity and turn it into a business."

"Thus, in our view, a critical aspect of being entrepreneurial has been the ability to negotiate the tension between the near term and the long term—between the immediate needs of customers and of the business divisions and the market opportunities that might arise when new technical capabilities are linked with the requirements of future customers."

"Lab managers used to be rewarded primarily for the quality of their research, which was measured for the most part by the technical community. We are now trying to cultivate a more business-oriented mind-set within the research and technology organization. . . . We are attempting to train and empower lab managers to function as well-grounded business people."

The Internet Start-Ups

The onset of the "Internet Start-up", sometimes referred to as dot.com's, has added a new dimension to the corporate culture. This "start-up" culture combines all of the above attributes, not because they are strategically focused on creating the "right" environment for employees, but because in order to "win" on the Internet, they have to. Time appears, at least at this point, to be the "start-ups'" biggest competitive threat. With time always against a company, decisions must be made immediately (decisions that could be fatal) and employees must be passionate about what they do because they are at it countless hours a week.

Many "brick and mortar" companies that are competing for a piece of the Internet pie are "spinning-out" separate divisions with very different cultures.

Take, for example, Procter and Gamble. A group of executives had a very bold idea. They wanted to start selling customized cosmetics to women via the Internet. The venture was to be named: reflect.com

The top brass started wondering how a far-flung $38 billion behemoth could best a flood of nimble, tech-savvy upstarts whose only mission in life is to win on the Web. They realized the answer was to become one of the nimble upstarts. "We wanted to create conditions common to the most successful Internet companies," says Denis Beausejour, P&G's worldwide vice-president of marketing for beauty care.

The result is a cyber-venture like no other. P&G is teaming up with Institutional Venture Partners, who is kicking in $15 million into the $50 million venture (and getting a 15% share). And now the upstart has been spun out into a separate entity, and reflect.com is moving to San Francisco. The dozen P&G employees were forced to resign from the parent company so they can could truly understand the risks of a startup. Many will take pay cuts for stock options.

Making An Innovation Culture Endure

By challenging employees to think, trust in themselves, and give them freedom to "run their own business," a manager creates a culture that stimulates and motivates employees to excel. (Running their own business means that every business action that an employee performs is done as if it were his or her own business.)

Based on information obtained from its annual survey of leading technology firms, The Industrial Research Institute has found systematic ways of promoting breakthroughs. The first is the ability to explain clearly to all employees, at every level, just how crucial the project is to the company's future. The second is to set next-to-impossible goals for those involved. The third is to target only "rich domains"—areas of investigation where plenty of answers are still waiting to be found. The fourth is to move people regularly between laboratories and business units, to ensure that researchers fully understand the needs of the marketplace.

Teresa Amabile suggests six managerial practices that can affect creativity:

1. Organizational Encouragement.—An organizational culture that encourages creativity through the fair, constructive judgment of ideas, reward and recognition for creative work, mechanisms for developing new ideas, an active flow of ideas, and a shared vision of what the organization is trying to do.

2. Supervisory Encouragement.—A supervisor who serves as a good work model, sets goals appropriately, supports the work group, values individual contributions, and shows confidence in the work group.

3. Work Group Supports.—A diversely skilled work group in which people communicate well, are open to new ideas, constructively challenge each other's work, trust and help each other, and feel committed to the work they are doing.

4. Sufficient Resources.—Access to appropriate resources, including funds, materials, facilities, and
information

5. Challenging Work. —A sense of having to work hard
on challenging tasks and important projects. *Of all the
things managers can do to stimulate creativity, perhaps the most efficacious is the deceptively simple
task of matching people with the right assignments.*

6. Freedom. —Freedom in deciding what work to do
and how to do it; a sense of control over one's work.
Freedom can easily be mismanaged. Managers tend to
change goals frequently or fail to clearly define them.

Amabile also outlines six procedures managers can use to
successfully spur and manage risk:

1. Show confidence in the team.

2. Ensure communication among team members is open
and free flowing.

3. Delegate management and/or task responsibility to
team members.

4. Provide appropriate resources.

5. Make sure each team member has challenging tasks.

6. Apply the right amount of pressure and tension.

A few steps companies are taking to create the attributes of
an "Internet Start-up" include:

✧ Eliminating layers of management

✧ Giving all employees a stake in the company

✧ Creating ways in which decisions can be made
faster

✧ Empowering employees

✧ Streamlining the "red-tape" (eliminating legal)
There are many "programs" or activities that can
be done to shape a mindset or culture.

In an innovative culture, employees don't "punch a clock," gossip at the water cooler, or ask questions like, "Why does Suzy get to . . . ?" Innovative cultures meet goals faster, have more breakthrough products, and enjoy higher returns than do their competitors. (Manager's also experience lower employee turnover.)

Managers loose site of the importance of accountability. By clearly defining expectations and deadlines and then "setting them free," employees take on an "I can do it" attitude and an air of ownership for success. The risk of fostering a culture that provides creativity, entrpreneurialism and freedom is that certain employees may somehow take advantage of the environment. Establishing accountability "weedsout" those employees. They don't last because they either are not willing to commit to goals or cannot meet them.

An important step in measuring a company culture starts with employee goals. By allowing employees to create their own goals, it automatically assigns accountability. Managers should then review the goals with them and come to a mutual agreement on what the employee is accountable for and expected to produce. Goals should include the initiative or project the employee is going to take on, the milestones or "tactics" that go with the project, deadlines, impact on the firm, and return on innovation investment (R2I).

Goals should be reviewed quarterly as it allows for employee freedom and creates a sense of urgency. Plus, managers can stay on top of employee activities without micro-managing. At the end of each quarter, managers should be able to aggregate an employee's goals and provide the "higher-ups" with a list of his or her department's accomplishments, costs, and impact on the firm.

Other ways managers can "measure" their departments success is to ask periodically (3–4 times a year) for each employee to provide a list of the top five initiatives they have introduced or implemented into the firm that have made a significant impact on revenues. Initiatives can be tangible or non-tangible. This reminds employees that everything they do should be adding to the firm's "bottom line." If your employees cannot provide a short list of impacts made—then guess what—they are not helping company revenues and are overhead.

In Summary

Fortune Magazine in 1999 declared the top 100 most innovative companies. These included Charles Schwab, Pfizer, Intel, Gillette, Corning, Lucent Technologies, Rubbermaid, Microsoft, Merck, Federal Express, Duke Energy, Home Depot, 3M, America Online and Procter & Gamble. What do these companies have in common? The following characteristics depict their cultures:

- ✦ Respect for individualism
- ✦ Permission to take risks
- ✦ Customer-focused and oriented
- ✦ Willing to invest in R&D and innovation
- ✦ Committed to making their people the best
- ✦ High energy level
- ✦ Positive, buoyant, "can-do" attitude
- ✦ A positive pro-active, confident, and respectful attitude that enables innovation to gestate and grow.

Index